"As a Reiki Master Teacher, I have purchased Reiki, many of which contain the same or sim Reiki: A Path of Inclusion' has some new and "being-ness" of Reiki. For John, Reiki is not si much more. Reiki is a way of life; a path to 'self empowerment, self awareness.' I highly recommend adding this book to your library. I found 'The Nature of Reiki' to be both thought provoking and inspiring."

Jane Van De Veld

"Thank you, thank you, thank you! I have been searching my whole life for a better understanding of spirituality. Finally someone makes sense of it all. I appreciate all you have done. Thank you again."

Jennifer Rietveld

"As a medical practitioner, my emphasis and education has been based in the traditional teachings of allopathic medicine. This book provides an excellent introduction to the understanding and practice of healing and balance through spiritual techniques. My connectedness to my patients and fellow health care providers has been enhanced as a result of your book."

James E. Beckett, MD

"'The Nature of Reiki' is a well-written, inspiring, and worldly insight into the beautiful healing energy of Reiki. This book provides useful tips to the trained Reiki practitioner as well as those who are exploring energy work for the first time. It brings the Love and light down to earth and yet keeps the pure wonderment. Would highly recommend."

Michelle Myers Doty

"This book has come at just the right time. John very adeptly supports the reader to realize how Reiki can be a part of everyday life. It's one of the few books out there that makes the reader want to incorporate the concepts immediately into their daily activity."

Robert Reilly

"'The Nature of Reiki: A Path of Inclusion' is the story of a great adventure. I loved the personal story of John David Sparks and Reiki. Unlike other Reiki books, this book allowed me to feel a passion and journey of another Reiki practitioner. So exciting! A very truthful story that opens Reiki to a way of life."

Sue Ellen Roberts

"The Nature of Reiki came into my life at a good time, actually anytime would be a good time for this book. I think this will be one of those books I refer to throughout life, to keep me BALANCED. I found it informative and a light read in this complicated world."

Jan Fitzgerald

The Nature of Reiki:
A Path of Inclusion

John David Sparks

BALBOA
PRESS
A DIVISION OF HAY HOUSE

Copyright © 2011 John David Sparks

All rights reserved. No part of this book may be used or reproduced by any means, graphic, electronic, or mechanical, including photocopying, recording, taping or by any information storage retrieval system without the written permission of the publisher except in the case of brief quotations embodied in critical articles and reviews.

Balboa Press books may be ordered through booksellers or by contacting:

Balboa Press
A Division of Hay House
1663 Liberty Drive
Bloomington, IN 47403
www.balboapress.com
1-(877) 407-4847

Because of the dynamic nature of the Internet, any web addresses or links contained in this book may have changed since publication and may no longer be valid. The views expressed in this work are solely those of the author and do not necessarily reflect the views of the publisher, and the publisher hereby disclaims any responsibility for them.

The author of this book does not dispense medical advice or prescribe the use of any technique as a form of treatment for physical, emotional, or medical problems without the advice of a physician, either directly or indirectly. The intent of the author is only to offer information of a general nature to help you in your quest for emotional and spiritual well-being. In the event you use any of the information in this book for yourself, which is your constitutional right, the author and the publisher assume no responsibility for your actions.

Cover design by Georgina Chapman
Hand Position photos by Valerie Reilly

ISBN: 978-1-4525-3574-6 (e)
ISBN: 978-1-4525-3573-9 (sc)

Library of Congress Control Number: 2011910287

Printed in the United States of America

Balboa Press rev. date: 8/16/2011

"Reiki is light and Love in motion. When we become aware that each and every cell of our body has within it the *Nature* of Reiki, our life shifts in phenomenal ways."

John David Sparks

CONTENTS

Preface ix

Acknowledgements xiii

REIKI: HEALING THE SELF THROUGH CONSCIOUSNESS EXPANSION

Hearing the Word.. 3

My Conscious Journey 7

The Story of Dr. Usui 15

The Origins of Reiki 21

Choices 33

Embracing Our Dark Side.. 39

Beliefs 45

Affirmations.. 51

    Affirmations for Physical Healing 55

    Affirmations for Fear of Change 56

    Affirmations for Love.. 57

    Affirmations for Loss and Grief............................... 59

    Affirmations for Abundance.................................... 61

    Affirmation for Self Worth...................................... 62

Intention 65

THE TECHNIQUES OF HEALING THROUGH REIKI

Getting Started "The Energy Body" 73

Working with Another "The Reiki Treatment" 75

    Hand Positions 78

    Exploring the Chakras and More 82

The Symbols 89

    Activating the Symbols 91

    The Power Symbol 92

    The Mental–Emotional Symbol 94

    The Distance Symbol 95

    The Master Symbol 98

    The Tibetan Symbols 99

Step by Step Session Instructions 101

    Physical Healing 101

    Emotional Healing 104

CONCLUSION: THE EVER PRESENT JOY OF REIKI

A Path of Inclusion 111

About the Author 115

Recommended Reading 117

PREFACE

There are many schools of Reiki, each with their own unique variations of approaching and using the life force energy. Throughout the years of my Reiki experience, I have watched its teachings shift and change as dedicated people around the world delve further into its truth. These truths have largely dealt with a more accurate history and techniques of the early masters not known in the beginning, particularly with the Usui System. Acknowledging this, I would like to clearly state that this book is <u>not</u> an attempt to write or re-write the story and history of Dr. Usui. There is speculation about the <u>possibility</u> of additional history, but there is also a clear reference to the documented history as it is known today. While this documented history is important to many people, it is not my focus or concern in this book. Though I have honored Dr. Usui because of his role in bringing Reiki to the world, this book is not about him or his techniques. It is about the <u>nature</u> of the energy itself, an energy which has existed long before the word Reiki was even conceived. In fact, it has existed since the beginning of time. This book is a very personal journey of my own search, understanding, and enfoldment into this ever expanding mystery of light and Love. Woven throughout its pages is the spiritual foundation I have come to believe is inherent in its nature. The literal translation of the word is very often glossed over without much thought. Yet, the experiential awareness of Reiki as the connecting thread to all life quickly brings a deeper understanding. Think about it. Through the innate intelligence and fundamental desire in life itself, we are always seeking, and always moving toward recreating ourselves as the next greatest version of who we are. This inherent desire to "be" it all is really the desire to merge with the Source from which we came; the All That Is, also known as God. Opening to and immersing ourselves in Reiki is opening to the nature of ourselves as a son or daughter of God. To think of Reiki without acknowledging its nature is to think of ourselves without acknowledging our <u>own</u> nature: That of Divinity Itself.

Historical facts and techniques are important for the mind, but the heart of Reiki is what changed my life and put this book in motion. The explosion of new symbols and systems over the past 15 to 20 years is a clear indication that new techniques will always be forthcoming. While they have served to expand the intellectual knowledge base of Reiki, I feel the nature and vastness of its character hasn't been addressed to the degree that I have felt it in my life. This nature is what underlies all the systems and approaches that have been or will be developed. We are all using the same life energy. By understanding its character and quality we enhance whatever system we may choose. By understanding the "Nature of Reiki" we can begin to understand the nature of ourselves since we are here only by the grace of that life force. So this is my contribution, my attempt at expressing and hopefully inspiring others to the joy that comes from this fundamental energy that permeates the universe. As we let go into this sea of Love that surrounds us we begin to feel a joyful connection to life itself. The undeniable beauty of opening to the Reiki energy can be more than a momentary feeling. It can be more than a one-day or two-day workshop. It can, if you choose, become a path. A path that has no boundaries, doctrines, or dogma that you must attach to it in order to find peace within yourself. Continuing to open to the life force brings about synchronistic events that encompass all areas of your life.

Would you like to fit the pieces of the puzzle together? To allow all religions, actions of your friends, and world situations to appear as perfection rather than chaos? Would you like to feel the beauty within your own heart and allow that beauty to express itself freely? These things are possible if we dedicate ourselves to them. The journey of life can become a never ending path of knowledge and mystery when we open to the energy of our own essence. It's time we realized that Reiki is more than a technique. It's the foundation of our existence. It's more than we can comprehend, yet it can be the doorway and path to an ever-evolving experience of ourselves as sons and daughters of God.

ACKNOWLEDGEMENTS

This book is the outpouring of an inner voice that wanted to speak. It would not have been possible were it not for the encouragement, guidance, support, and love offered by people throughout my life. My gratitude extends beyond those who are mentioned here, but for the sake of sparing the reader endless pages of unfamiliar names, I have limited my acknowledgements to those most closely connected to my journey. First, I'd like to thank my Reiki teacher William Rand. His wisdom, patience, understanding, and passionate desire to help make the world a better place revitalized my path of self discovery and opened new doors of insight.

I would also like to thank my wife Kathleen, and friends Valerie Reilly, Sue Ellen Roberts, Judith Monahan, Penny Will, Terry Cunningham, and Teresa Weis. For his time, heart, and expertise in the Chinese interpretation of the symbols, my profound gratitude is extended to Dr. Ming Te Lin . A special thank you to Peggy Brown, Valerie Reilly, and Robert Reilly for meticulously combing through my words and putting them into type. For inspiration and guidance I would like to thank Paramahansa Yogananda, Babaji, Jesus, Sadhguru Jaggi Vesudev, the Brotherhood for Healing, and Ariannah.

And last but not least, all those who have knowingly or unknowingly supported or helped me find an inner strength and purpose to my life. Not the least of which is my immediate family, students, clients, and all my friends through the years. Thank you.

REIKI:
HEALING THE SELF THROUGH
CONSCIOUSNESS EXPANSION

HEARING THE WORD

"In the beginning was the Word; and the Word was with God;
and the Word was God."
John 1:1 - King James Bible

The word of God is the sound of creation. It contains within it the inseparable quality of the life force. Reiki is a Japanese word which, when translated, means Universal Life Force Energy. This soundless sound, or word of God, is the causative vibration of light and Love that has always been and always will be, it is light and Love in motion. In a sense, Reiki is the word of God.

The Chinese ttranslation of the same kanji (or characters) that create the concept Reiki is "life force energy from beyond the beyond". In other words, life force from a place beyond intellectual conception. Its balance and intelligence can be easily seen by observing the life pattern of anything from an amoeba to a galaxy and everything in between. Take, for example, the human body. It is so complex that science is involved in an ever-expanding study of how it works. Did you ever notice that there is no end to this study? No matter how advanced our technology becomes, the mystery of how the life force interpenetrates, revitalizes, regenerates, connects, and balances the trillions and trillions of cells in our body's remains beyond our understanding. Studying

THE NATURE OF REIKI: A PATH OF INCLUSION

the effects of these complex interactions is a fascinating, yet endless pursuit.

Sometimes it appears that an imbalance within the system has taken place which can lead to all manner of physical and emotional problems. Typically, the field of health care will investigate the effects or symptoms of this imbalance and seek to stabilize it. The result is an ever-expanding array of approaches, such as drugs, technology and modalities to deal with the situation. Even holistic or alternative health care practitioners are often focused on the effects. Instead of a prescription drug, vitamins or nutrients of some sort are commonly offered. Perhaps balance is found through various modalities like massage, Thai Bodywork, QiGong, Reiki, Craniosacral Therapy or Chiropractic. These are all wonderful ways to bring ourselves back to homeostasis[1]. It cannot be denied that these methods can be effective.

In fact, I remember a personal incident when I had an illness that brought moderate fear into my life. My initial visit to the doctor suggested I get a biopsy and prepare for an operation. The thought of becoming part of the medical system sent shudders down my spine. I decided I would try to heal myself. I struggled to overcome my problem using every modality I knew. Two or three months went by to no avail. The pain was as severe as it had been from the onset. Frightened and confused as to why I had not been able to heal myself, I sought counsel from a gifted friend of mine who acted as a channel for "higher" information to be vocalized through her. When asked what I could do to demonstrate a healing, the reply was a surprise. "Go to a doctor you feel comfortable with, and let them take some of the burden from you. You have been trying too hard and just need to release some of your concern to someone you trust, and in the space of allowing, your healing will occur much faster." I felt relief as I heard the message. It immediately resonated as true.

---

1 Homeostasis: The process by which the body stays in balance.

HEARING THE WORD

I promptly sought out a holistic chiropractic physician and began treatment. Within a couple of months I was feeling less pain and a lot less fear. But more importantly, I now had space to explore the mental and emotional issues that surrounded and created my illness in the first place. In this way I moved toward a vibrational shift that was complete and my healing permanent. I believe that when we use the help available to us we can more easily move into alignment with the life force that animates our being. Let me be clear about my gratitude regarding modern allopathic medicine and the broad spectrum of alternative approaches. They have served us well in many ways. Countless ailments and even disease have been eradicated because of the dedicated individuals researching how the physical body works. My heartfelt thanks goes to them all.

Yet, all too often, even in alternative and holistic practices, I see people who just want to be "fixed". They want someone else to do the work for them without ever spending time with themselves. The problem with this is that unless we are able to genuinely shift the root of the problem it will continue to manifest. It may look a little different the next time, but rest assured that until we address the block inhibiting the life force (Reiki) from moving freely through our body/mind, we will continue to be plagued. Trying to escape this truth often leads the person from one modality to another, creating a storyline all its own which keeps him or her from addressing core issues.

Please notice that I have not stated we have to find the root of the problem, only that we have to shift it from a very deep place. We may or may not be able to discover the root of our illness. In fact, sometimes as we tunnel back to the past, we end up getting caught in more and more pain since that is where we are focused. If you feel it necessary to journey into the past to heal the present, do so with clear intention and a watchful eye.

For those searching for something different than endless techniques, claiming one is more powerful than the next, perhaps a dip into

THE NATURE OF REIKI: A PATH OF INCLUSION

Source itself will serve us in working from a place beyond intellectual understanding; a place where the journey itself brings healing while we are gently guided to the next step; a place where the flow of life force carries us peacefully into the arms of God. "For man shall not live by bread alone but by every word that proceedeth out of the mouth of God"[2]. In other words, our life is not sustained only by the physical care we give it, but also by the full spectrum of life force energy emanating from Source[3], or God. In his book, *Friendship with God*, Neale Donald Walsch quotes God as saying "God is the life force energy turned all the way up!"[4]

What if we begin to think of Reiki as the essence of who we are? After all, doesn't the life force permeate every cell of our being? What if we could align our consciousness with the intelligent consciousness of the life force? What if Reiki were more than a hands-on healing technique and we could use it to expand into greater awareness? What if the possibilities of our limited self could be expanded to the unlimited self? Would you want to take the journey? If you answered yes, I invite you to enjoy looking at a new view of the history of this gentle but powerful force. You'll soon discover that its known history beckons an inquiry into its use long before Dr. Usui, who is credited with bringing Reiki to the modern world in the early 1900's. If you answered no, and you just want to learn more about the "hands-on" aspect of using it, I invite you to continue, for that too is covered in detail.

In either case, perhaps you will be able to answer the question, "what is Reiki?" from an experiential and personal place after you have opened to the concepts and exercises offered in this book. Truly, your experience is the only way to understand it.

---

2   Mathew 4:4, King James version – Scofield Reference Bible
3   Source – Referring to the ultimate source from which all life was given expression.
4   Hampton Roads Publishing

MY CONSCIOUS JOURNEY

"The church says the earth is flat;
but I have seen its shadow on the moon,
and I have more confidence even in
a shadow than in the church."
Ferdinand Magellan

In the spring of 1991, I was preparing to graduate from massage school. All the students in my class had become like a family to me. We had worked on each other for months and shared much about ourselves. This was due in part to the way the school was organized. Not only was there an instructor for the various components involved in massage therapy, there was also a psychologist who worked with us as a group.

It was a turning point in my life. I had studied metaphysics since the early 1970's and found great value and comfort in learning to approach life from the perspective of Eastern and Western mystics. Oddly enough, all of my study had not brought me to the doorway of knowing my own body, nor had it brought me peace. This incredible miracle that I walked around in every day was a stranger to me. I discovered my body had cellular memory and that it had emotional wounds buried deep within it. I discovered that I loved nurturing other human beings and loved being nurtured. In short, I discovered I was feeling more in touch with my own body than ever before, more grounded, and much more alive. I certainly had a childlike sense of anticipation in what awaited me after graduation. I was anxious to explore all doors of opportunity. So when one of my classmates engaged me in a conversation about Reiki one night after class I was thoroughly intrigued.

"Have you heard of Reiki?" she asked. "No" I answered, not even sure I had heard the name correctly. "Well, I hadn't either," she replied. "But when I was at a spiritual retreat in Wisconsin I decided to try a treatment. I still don't know how to explain it but I can tell you that it felt like I was floating outside of my body for forty-five minutes. It was awesome!"

I nodded my head as if I understood but let the conversation drop. I knew there were no words to communicate the deep feelings connected with such an experience. Then, a couple of weeks later, she approached me again. "I understand there's a Reiki Master coming to Indiana in June. Would you like to take the class with me?" she inquired. "Sure," I replied, not knowing why. Although I now know that life is always calling us to play and expand in the ever deepening understanding of who we are. When we are open to it, we will feel it tapping us on the shoulder.

As fate would have it, I seemed to have been overlooked when it came to the mailing of strongly advised considerations prior to class. My teacher believed it beneficial to abstain from, or at least cut down on, the intake of meat, alcohol, sugar, chocolate, caffeine and other heavy or stimulating foods. He advised more quiet time or meditation for the week prior to class.

Of course, not having received this information, I walked in with my Dunkin Donuts "Big One" cup of coffee. Then I found out that each person was supposed to have brought a dish of food to be shared at lunch. I stopped at the local grocery after class that evening and picked up some chocolate brownies for the next day before going to my brother-in-law's birthday bash. I probably don't need to tell you I had little reservation about consuming alcohol that evening.

That next day at class I proudly displayed the brownies to everyone's delight except the teacher. "No, anything but chocolate!", I remember him saying. Well, he finally softened, saying that it wasn't the worst thing in the world, but told us to wait until after class before eating them.

To say that my body was clogged with toxins requires no great insight. It therefore probably won't surprise anyone when I say I could not feel the energy flow of Reiki moving through me, even at the end of day two (the second level attunement). Were it not for two things that occurred during class, I would have thought that I just wasted my money and my time.

During the level one attunement I saw in my mind's eye and felt myself undergoing the same, or very similar, attunement and ritual back in ancient Egypt. I had the uncanny feeling that even some of the same people were present. This provided a deep sense of connection for me and made me ponder its origins and my past.

On the second day we were led on a journey to meet our Reiki Master. Not being a person who considers himself a good visualizer, I had a difficult time with some aspects of the process. I didn't see things in great detail, but I did see general outlines. More importantly for me though, I had deep, deep feelings about what I did see. The Love my Reiki Master imparted upon me brought me out of this meditation in tears. I was overwhelmed. I knew I had been given a great gift, and this experience seemed to validate the class for me.

Three days later, the flood gates were opened as the Reiki energy finally worked its way through the clogs and found an outlet through my palms. I'll never forget how good it felt playing with a giant energy ball between my hands, or how startled my co-workers were as they felt the heat radiating out of my hands. "My God, it feels like the sun," was

THE NATURE OF REIKI: A PATH OF INCLUSION

the first comment. From then on I was hooked. I began using it more and more with my massage treatments, getting good to great results. After about a year, when my confidence level was pretty high, I ran into a personal challenge of fear.

While giving on-site chair massage at a hospital sponsored wellness day, I ran into another massage therapist who had been using Reiki but decided to quit. I couldn't understand why anyone would quit using it, so I asked what had made her come to this decision. She answered nonchalantly saying it was too long of a story to explain right now, but if I wanted to call her at home, she would explain. A few days passed before I called her, but she was still hesitant to talk about it. "I should really talk to you in person," she said. "I don't think I can explain it very well on the phone." Now my curiosity was peaked. I was preparing to go for the advanced Reiki class and if there was something I needed to know, I wanted to know now before I spent any more time and money. So we arranged a meeting for lunch, and she began to tell me her story with a sense of great gravity.

"I was using Reiki until I went to a well known school for energy work. This man was extremely intuitive and psychically advanced. He said that within the Reiki ray, as it connected to the crown chakra, was an almost imperceptible black thread. This thread, he explained, is connected to the masters of the dark side. And when one had undergone the higher initiations of Reiki, it strengthened this link and allowed these masters of the dark to take control of your soul." She went on to explain a couple of stories and questions which seemed to justify the story.

Although I can laugh at this story now, I must admit it threw me into a state of fear and panic. "Oh my God, what had I done? What had I been working with?" All the fear of thirty-nine years (and probably countless lifetimes) arose within me as I struggled to understand this dark thread. Could masters of the dark side really use the light to control me? Was there really such a thing as masters of the dark? Why was no one else able to see this thread? Why had I never felt the darkness? What about all the healings, the great feedback? Did masters of the dark perform healings too? If so, was it all an illusion so they could snap up my soul?

I pondered these questions day and night for about three weeks as fear slowly gave way to truth. If there really was a darkness, a force which battled the existence of light, a force which divides and destroys, why does the universe itself seem perfectly balanced? Why had it not destroyed itself long ago? I reasoned that when I was divided against myself I could not function properly. I had often become ill from this. Wasn't I a microcosmic example of universal order?

Abraham Lincoln's famous statement, "a house divided against itself cannot stand," has been embraced as a mighty truth that America stands on. Was it only true with regard to slavery? What about the healings, the awakenings? I could find no evidence that light turned to darkness with any of my clients. Finally I thought, what about *my* feelings? I may not be psychic or possess a great deal of esoteric knowledge, but I do have a great capacity for feeling. If I let go of the statement that caused the fear, what did I feel? I meditated and prayed, trying to get clear so I could feel the energies without the blinders of fear.

I finally realized that when I turn on the light, the darkness disappears. The darkness does indeed co-exist with the light, for when I turn it off the darkness reappears. It was up to me to turn the switch if I wanted light, and in this case the switch was Reiki. It was also up to me to realize that darkness didn't mean evil. It was simply a polarity, not unlike electricity which requires both a negative and positive pole (thus the black and white wires) to produce its current. Did "dark" have to mean "evil"? Did this person actually see a dark thread in the first place? It began to seem much more likely to me that his "sight" might have more to do with his own agenda than his vision of Reiki.

THE NATURE OF REIKI: A PATH OF INCLUSION

I moved forward in my training, accepting my own feelings of truth. This was a major step in gaining personal power. How often do we accept the authority of another and freeze our growth with fear?

My sessions became more and more powerful and situations in my life were beginning to change for the better. I had learned that Reiki was NOT connected to a "dark" force and there was nothing to fear. But what WAS Reiki? I had read the definitions over and over again, but it wasn't enough. So after about a year of working with the higher vibrational energies of the Usui master symbol, I decided to go for my "Master/Teacher" training held in Estes Park, Colorado. I had no idea how this would impact my life, but from the moment I began my journey, I felt the Universal Guidance directing my life. Who knows, maybe it was the mountains, maybe the fresh air, or maybe the Reiki training, but I have a feeling it was my enhanced ability as a result of the training to connect with the beauty of life itself that kept a huge smile plastered on my face.

When the training was over, I still couldn't answer the question of what Reiki was, but I was gaining a new appreciation of its mystery and its beauty. Such a powerful force called forth by our intent, connecting us to the beauty of this earth and realms beyond this world. Its power surged through my life, creating opportunities beyond my dreams. The people I began to connect with changed my life forever. Insight Awareness, my current livelihood, was opened as a result of a personal loan that one of my students offered me without ever asking for it.

I've now traveled nationally and internationally speaking on this ever expanding energy of universal beauty. Regularly scheduled classes continue to be offered in the Chicago area at Insight Awareness with co-teacher and business partner Valerie Reilly. And though the miracles continue to this day, I must admit that some of them have been realized by walking through the dark tunnels of my own soul.

MY CONSCIOUS JOURNEY

We'll get to that later, but for now, let's start with the story of Dr. Usui. As I mentioned earlier, Dr. Usui is credited with making the Reiki energies available to most of the modern world. Part of the beauty that Reiki training offers us is that anyone, even those of us brought up in the western culture, regardless of age or background, can learn how to use it.

THE STORY OF DR. USUI

"Neglect not the gift that is in thee, which was given thee by prophecy, with the laying on of hands."
1ˢᵗ Timothy 4:14 – King James Bible

Until her death in 1980, Mrs. Takata, the Japanese/American who introduced Reiki to the western world, told the only story of how Dr. Usui, a Japanese spiritualist, discovered Reiki back in the early 1900's.

In her classes and on audio tapes[5], Mrs. Takata weaves a liberal story of fiction and fact of how Dr. Usui embraced Christianity when it was introduced in Japan at the turn of the 20ᵗʰ century. It was a time of great change for political, economic and spiritual values. When the western missionaries discovered an open door, they naturally took advantage of the opportunity. According to Mrs. Takata, Dr. Usui was one of the few Buddhists in Japan that embraced these teachings.

Mrs. Takata said that he studied very hard to eventually become the dean of a small Christian College outside of Kyoto. It was there that a student asked him a question that changed his life. "Dr. Usui", the student inquired, "if you believe that the Bible speaks the truth when Jesus claimed that we could all do what he has done[6], could you teach

---

5   Mrs. Takata's tapes are available through The International Center for Reiki Training, Vision Publications.

6   John 14:12 – King James version – Scofield Reference Bible

THE NATURE OF REIKI: A PATH OF INCLUSION

us to heal?" Dr. Usui took the question to heart. He believed what the Bible said, but could not teach people to heal. He resigned from his post and dedicated his life to finding the answer to that question.

Finally, after years of traveling far and wide, including seven years at the University of Chicago studying Christian scripture, and various places in the East studying Buddhist scripture, he had an enlightened moment on top of Mt. Kurama (in Japan), while he was on a 21 day retreat. In an out-of-body experience he saw multi-colored, translucent bubbles containing the Reiki symbols. Meditating on them he became intimately acquainted, or attuned, to their innermost meaning. He also intuited a way in which he could impart that meaning to others, in a non-verbal way, without diluting their power. After he integrated his experience he began his healing work in the beggars' quarters of Kyoto, and eventually throughout much of Japan. He incorporated five principles which he called the **Reiki Ideals** as a foundation for offering healing. They are as follows:

1. *For today, don't be angry.*
2. *Do not worry.*
3. *Be grateful.*
4. *Work hard.* *(Relative to inner work)*
5. *Be kind to others.*

Eventually he taught sixteen dedicated men the secrets of his knowledge and power. These men were called Reiki Masters.

Mrs. Takata's story goes on to tell about Dr. Hayashi, a retired naval officer and mystic who had become one of Dr. Usui's students. Deeply honoring his path and the Reiki energy itself, Dr. Hayashi was committed to spreading the word and making sure the Reiki knowledge was never lost again. Dr. Hayashi eventually opened a Reiki clinic in Tokyo and established the system, or levels of Reiki training, with which we are familiar today. *The Hayashi Manual,*[7] by Frank Petter,

---

7   Frank Petter, Tadao Yamaguchi and Chujiro Hayashi, The Hayashi Manual,

THE STORY OF DR. USUI

Tadao Yamaguchi and Chujiro Hayashi, is a wonderful book detailing Dr. Hayashi's contribution to Reiki.

It was at this clinic that Mrs. Takata was introduced to Reiki. Although born in Hawaii, and still residing there, she had come back to Japan to visit her parents and inform them of her sister's death. While on this visit she was admitted to the hospital because of a long bout with upper respiratory problems, depression and a tumor in her abdomen. At the hospital it was determined that the tumor needed to be removed by surgery. Her intriguing tale of how she was led to the Reiki Clinic is one I have enjoyed telling to students over the years.

"Lying on the operating table in a room by myself," she states, "I heard a voice that said 'The operation is not necessary.' Looking around the room I began to feel fear as there was no one around when I heard the voice again, this time just a bit louder, 'The operation is not necessary,' it stated again. Then I really became afraid, wondering what I should do when the voice spoke again even louder. 'The operation is not necessary!' This time I sat up, pulled the I.V. out of my arm, wrapped the sheet around myself and went to find my surgeon. Sensing the fears within me he listened to my question with full attention and without judgment. 'Doctor, is there any way I can have my healing without the operation?' I asked." As it so happened, he knew Dr. Hayashi and suggested that she try his Reiki Clinic.

The rest, as they say, is history. After her admission she began to slowly heal. It was a four month process of being treated two times daily by two practitioners. Her fascination with what they were doing and how long they were doing it began to grow with great intensity. By the time she was ready to leave she had convinced Dr. Hayashi to teach her Reiki. This was something that no one expected, since it had never been taught to a woman before and because, even though she was of Japanese descent, being born in Hawaii, she was looked upon as

---

Lotus Press, Shanghi La Publishing, ISBN#0-914955-75-6

THE NATURE OF REIKI: A PATH OF INCLUSION

being a foreigner. The Japanese wanted to keep this healing art within their own culture.

Nonetheless, her sincerity convinced Dr. Hayashi that she would be just the right person to teach. He had sensed a great war on the horizon and knew the possibility existed that if only men knew Reiki, the knowledge of how to use it may be lost again in the rubble of war. A woman, on the other hand, would not be fighting in battle. Though there was always the chance of civilian casualties, even that was reduced because Mrs. Takata would be living in Hawaii.

Mrs. Takata worked in the Reiki clinic for a year and then went back to Hawaii in 1937 where Dr. Hayashi and his daughter helped her set up her practice. In 1938 Dr. Hayashi initiated her as a Reiki Master and, through heart-felt determination and very clever practices, she was able to spread the teachings of Reiki throughout the West. One of her most clever ideas, which was mentioned at the beginning of this story, was to create a bit of a myth around the history of Dr. Usui as a Christian. You see, around the time she was trying to get her practice established in Hawaii, there was growing hostility toward the Japanese people. World War II was on the horizon and anything associated with Japan was not looked on favorably. It is my belief that because of this entrenched mindset, and make no mistake these were very fearful times, she created the history of Dr. Usui with a Christian background. Mrs. Takata knew that in this way it at least stood a chance of acceptability.

For quite a few years, even after her death in 1980, no one questioned her version of Reiki's history. Then in 1990, in hopes of finding out more about Dr. Usui, William Rand began researching his life based on Mrs. Takata's story. What he began to uncover was in great contrast to what he had been taught. Since then, William Rand, Frank Arjava Petter, and others have done an incredible job of creating a more accurate history about Dr. Usui, Dr. Hayashi, and the tradition of Japanese Reiki. I would recommend their books to anyone seeking to

THE STORY OF DR. USUI

explore Reiki's written history. You will find these books listed in the back.

An abbreviated version of the new history honors Dr. Usui as a humble man and a great healer. Throughout his life he searched for ways to improve the body and mind, just for the sake of becoming a better person. This pursuit led him to Europe, China, and some believe Tibet, to study medicine, psychology, religion and fortune telling.

Married with two children, he worked very hard in his own business, which despite his numerous gifts, eventually struggled and failed. Greatly upset, he decided to go to Mt. Kurama where he had received his early Buddhist training, and enrolled in a 21 day spiritual retreat. By fasting, meditating and praying, he hoped to find answers to his struggling life. During this time he had a satori[8], or sudden awakening. It's not known for sure how this occurred, but a widely accepted possibility is that a meditation under a waterfall opened his crown chakra allowing a powerful rush of Reiki energy to enter his body. This may indeed be true, as it was common practice for many to sit under the waterfall.

After his satori he opened his own Reiki Clinic in Tokyo and began a healing society called the Usui Reiki Ryoho Gakkai. During his time there he treated thousands of patients, including many from the great Tokyo earthquake in 1923. His reputation as a healer became widely recognized, even by the government. In March of 1926 he suffered a fatal stroke while teaching Reiki.

It's interesting to note here that of the many stories about Dr. Usui, a great amount of emphasis was once placed around his supposed travels to Tibet. Arthur Robertson and others once taught that his moment of awakening was most likely the result of a holy sutra[9] he discovered while in Tibet. And while a more accurate history of his life has been

---

8   Satori – Enlightenment; the word literally means "understanding."

9   Sutra – A sanskrit word referring to the concise meaning of a literary composition in spiritual teachings.

THE NATURE OF REIKI: A PATH OF INCLUSION

pieced together since the death of Mrs. Takata, there are still many details missing. For example, where in Europe and China did he study? And, isn't it entirely possible that when in China he visited Tibet? If not, then what was the basis of those stories?

I asked a gifted channel, Judith Monahan, who channels a group of souls called The Brotherhood for Healing, about Dr. Usui's travels to Tibet. I offer their words here only because they resonated deep inside of me as true, and if true, open the door for vast inquiry. They, The Brotherhood for Healing, said that Dr. Usui had studied with Tibetan Masters and learned the foundation of meditation techniques that led to his awakening back in Japan. Whether or not it was under a waterfall we'll never know for sure. But one thing seems clear, the Tibetans had been using the life force energy that Dr. Usui called "Reiki" long before it became popularized.

Let's take a look at how Reiki may have been anchored and used on our planet prior to Dr. Usui.

THE ORIGINS OF REIKI

"Reiki is the omnipresent Life Force of the universe through which the
intention of light and Love is given expression."
John David Sparks

Our planet is so beautiful! Its mysteries have captivated the greatest minds in every civilization. Its grandeur has captivated the heart of every lover. Countless civilizations have come and gone leaving behind legends that ignite our imagination. Of all that remains, the essence of what continues to touch our hearts through their art, structures, and symbols is Love. Love is the core and essence of who we are. Love is the essence of life.

Given that Reiki is the life force of the universe, it's not much of a stretch to realize that Reiki has always existed on our planet. In fact, our planet wouldn't exist without Reiki. All of the plants, animals, and even what we call inanimate objects have a life force at their core which sustains the very atoms of their existence. There have always been advanced souls on our planet that were aware of, and used, the Reiki energies. Gifted seers and prophets, such as Edgar Cayce and Solara, talk about these souls and their role in preparing the earth for the future civilizations.

THE NATURE OF REIKI: A PATH OF INCLUSION

Legends of these ancient ones are still a part of indigenous cultures. They speak of the Gods who walked among them coaxing plant life out of the earth and converting the elements of the earth to the form of jewelry and precious stone. Of "molding" giant blocks of stone to fit like jigsaw puzzles into walls, and of honoring the cycles of our earth within the celestial scheme of time. These things and more have likely been part of an inheritance which we are just now beginning to acknowledge.

While volumes of information, most of which are frowned on by North American scientists, are available for helping piece together our planet's incredible history, there seems to be a reoccurring thread that runs through them all - the connection to divinity. This is the essence of Reiki, the connection, or bridge, between the visible and the invisible; between the manifest and the un-manifest, between matter and spirit. Reiki is the bridge for continually expanding our consciousness into the infinite mind of God or "All that Is". Contemplating Reiki in this way helps us to understand that this energy has a much greater capacity than we are currently acknowledging. Is it not plausible that the ancient ones used the Reiki energy to connect to and work in harmony with the life force inherent in our planet to produce crops, create precision walls of stone, and more? Modern science has proven that matter is not solid. Quantum physicists speculate that mind creates matter. By opening to greater amounts of Reiki in our life, we connect with the omnipresent Life Force of the universe through which the intention of light and Love are given expression. By aligning our intention with the nature of Reiki, (life, light, Love, peace, power, beauty, joy, and abundance), it may be possible to rearrange sub-atomic particles in a way that not only alters our normal perception, but also the arrangement of matter itself.

Let's take a look at how Reiki, in its expanded definition, may have been used by some of the more notable people through history.

22

THE ORIGINS OF REIKI

EGYPT

From my experience during my first attunement, I believe the ancient Egyptians knew how to use the spiritually guided life force that today we call Reiki; perhaps not all the Egyptians, but the community of priests and priestesses for sure. My memory of initiation in that land was only strengthened when I visited there on New Year 2000, the change of millennium. I could imagine no other place on the planet I'd rather have been. The symbol of The Great Pyramid, as depicting the consciousness of man, was strong within me. Where else could I visit the past and the future at the same time? Memories rose within me of times before recorded history. Times of lush green vegetation in the area where the sacredness of life was a given. At night in my dreams I was "downloaded" with scroll after scroll of hieroglyphic text reacquainting me with my time and connection to this ancient land. Last, but not least, was another initiation inside The Great Pyramid. My friend and business partner at that time, Sue Ellen Roberts, went into a trance inside the Queens Chamber and placed her hands on the sides of my head. I felt currents of energy moving from one side of my head to the other. In my mind's eye it appeared like horizontal arcs of light in a science laboratory. Occasionally she would place a hand on my heart as if connecting those centers together. When complete, I felt as though I had been re-wired to accept the energies of the coming times. Indeed, a new millennium had dawned within me.

What I realized was that the ancient Egyptians used Reiki for consciousness expansion to transcend the concept of death. Many people believe they were obsessed with death, but in truth (as I experienced it), they were passionate about understanding and experiencing eternal life. It's interesting to note the similarities of the Egyptian symbol of eternal life, the ankh, with the Christian symbol of the cross on which Jesus died proclaiming an eternal life. At the time when the Great Pyramid was being built, the community of priests and priestesses were using Reiki in many ways that we are largely unfamiliar with today. Hands-on-healing was not the main focus because in their evolved community there was no one to heal. When the Pharaohs and others outside their community heard that these priests and priestesses were learning to conquer death they did not fully understand. It was customary for every ruler to have a priest as an advisor. When they heard that these priests wanted to use the pyramid as a way to transcend death they began using them as burial chambers, except one – The Great Pyramid. While it contained a sarcophagus in the King's Chamber, no body was ever found. It is my belief that this great, unbelievably precise structure was an initiation chamber for those who qualified to study and experience eternal life before physical death. They developed techniques and philosophies that allowed them to travel in the ever expanding energies of the universal life force, and experience the freedom beyond the physical body and ego mind. Like every evolved spirit, they came to know that what we call death is an illusion.

TIBET

In a similar fashion, but without the symbolism of a pyramid, the ancient Tibetans used Reiki for both consciousness expansion and physical healing. Initiation for opening into the boundless life force was reserved for an elite few who understood the concept of oneness beyond intellectual speculation. Of course it wasn't called Reiki, and the symbols weren't Japanese, but if we know nothing else of the Tibetan culture, we know that they were, and are, a culture dedicated to oneness. What better way to realize the fullness of that connection than through the opening of our life energy into the Source from which it came?

As mentioned earlier, the history of Dr. Usui and his travels used to include a tribute to Tibet. Not being able to trace the written confirmation of these stories, it has been deleted. Whether the origins of these stories are accurate or not may always be in question, but by

THE ORIGINS OF REIKI

revisiting the stories we may get a clue about the way Reiki was used there.

It is written that the Tibetan Lamas originally used Reiki as a system of meditation. Sacred symbols depicting aspects of the universal life force were painted on large wall hangings and were the central focus of the meditation. A monk would sit on a four legged stool in the center of an earthenware container which was filled with about three inches of water. The container was oval in shape to represent the ethereal egg of light which surrounds us. The stool was made of wood with a pure silver inlay going in a channel up each leg of the stool and connecting with a silver cubical inlay symbol upon the seat. One wall of the room was made of highly polished copper towards which the monk faced. Behind the monk were sacred symbols on the wall hangings which were reflected by the copper wall. By meditating on the symbols, their essence became implanted in the subconscious mind thereby raising consciousness and the overall physical vibration of the body. The polished copper wall reflected not only the sacred symbols, but also the fact that the symbols were only a reflection of the truth. All seekers of truth come to understand the reflective quality of life mirroring to them a deeper meaning.

It is also believed by some that the Tibetans understood and used the vibrational quality inherent in the symbols for physical healing. By holding the vibration of the symbol that would balance the imbalance of disease, the monk could help alleviate illness. It is believed that the symbol inlaid upon the wooden stool used for meditation was one of the most powerful symbols for alleviating almost any illness.

However, acquiring the ability to hold its vibration was no easy task since the symbol has multi-dimensional qualities. This symbol is most commonly known as the Antahkarana. It does not appear to be Tibetan in origin and therefore not part of what we in the west have come to know as Reiki. My own research indicates the symbol predates

THE NATURE OF REIKI: A PATH OF INCLUSION

the Tibetans and is part of twelve master symbols which will become available as our consciousness is ready to work with them. This symbol in particular, the Antahkarana, is a very earth oriented symbol and assists us in grounding and magnifying energies.

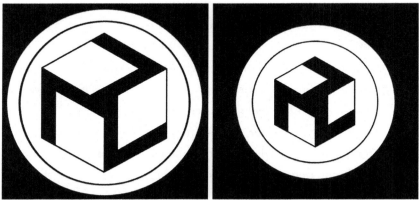

Female Antahkarana   Male Antahkarana

The Rosicrucian's, an ancient order of spiritual seekers, call the Antahkarana the psychic bridge that connects the physical brain and its psychic counterpart to our higher consciousness. This is very fitting, when you consider the multi-dimensional qualities of the Antahkarana.

As an earth symbol, the Antahkarana can be very important in bridging our awareness to understand the oneness we have with our planet. If there were ever a time to bring this awareness out from hiding, it is now. Our connection to this earth is so much more than we, as a collective consciousness, have ever realized before. If we each do our part we can still have a home. Use the Antahkarana to bring about this awakening. Meditate on it. Place the image over a map or globe and send the Reiki energies through it for healing. Visualize it spinning within the core of the planet emanating its powerful energy around the globe. Sit on it while you meditate and send the energies out through the bottoms of your feet. Use it any way your imagination comes up with. Remember, intention is always the key. While there may have been more ways the Tibetans used the Reiki energies, suffice it to say that their knowledge of the energy was likely the foundation that gave strength to Dr. Usui's meditation on Mt. Kurama.

It is also interesting to note that, if true, this information would have been taken out of Tibet a relatively short time before the Chinese invasion. Since then, more than 15,000 temples have been destroyed along with sacred texts and artifacts, not to mention the Tibetan way of life. In my view, the timing of this event and the role that Reiki has played in grounding the energies for the coming age have been perfect and invaluable.

JESUS

Probably the most noted healer in history was Jesus the Christ. There is much to consider here with the way in which he utilized the life force energy. By taking a closer look at his ministry, we can apply the truths he exposed to create a more powerful healing vortex in our own work. As he said, "He that believeth in me, the works that I do shall he do also; and greater works than these shall he do; because I go unto my father."[10]

Jesus was a man of vision. He dreamt of opening his heart to the heart of God which is the heart of all mankind. He dreamt of living in a way that was so impeccable that no one could knock him off his feet. Jesus dreamt of planting a seed that offered hope and inspiration to humanity. He dreamt of a Love so vast that it would absorb him until he became Love itself, and so it was. Jesus the man, became the Christ, or embodiment of Love which is the "only begotten" son of God. In other words, the only offspring of God is absolute Love. The path of his ministry was first the path to Self.

Let's take a look at this path, which we will call the Reiki path, since it is the path of opening to a greater union of light and Love in motion.

---

10   John 14:12 – King James version – Scofield Reference Bible

THE NATURE OF REIKI: A PATH OF INCLUSION

The first thing to acknowledge is our vision. For it is our vision, our dream, that will lead us to the next door of our evolution. Even a Reiki attunement, the powerful process of opening our energy centers to the Divine, would not be possible if we did not have that vision within us. So, dream. Dream of the possibilities that Jesus spoke of, the possibility that we are truly one with the creator. That being made in the likeness and image of God makes all things possible. Dream of how you might want to live, work, and be in this world of unlimited opportunity. Read the great works of divine inspiration by whoever inspires you, and know that they all spring from the foundation of opening to the greater and ever expanding awareness of the life force energy we call Reiki.

It is believed by many that Jesus' mother, Mary, and earthly father, Joseph, belonged to an elite sect of scholars known as the Essenes. This mysterious group of advanced souls date back to 500 years before the birth of Christ through the teachings found in the Dead Sea Scrolls. It is known that various sects of the Essenes include the Nazarenes and the Ebionites. The Essenes viewed prayer as a language to honor heaven and earth and created no separation between them. Phrases like "Our Father in Heaven", and "our Mother Earth" give us a clue to the concepts these great souls embraced as a part of their everyday life.

It is likely that Jesus was trained in the way of the Essenes since birth. The spiritual insights made available to him supported his beliefs until they became a knowing. At a young age this knowing guided him to study with the great spiritual masters of his time. Prophets such as Edgar Cayce offer possible insights into this time which has become known as the lost years of Jesus. It was during this time of extensive study that the mantle of the Christ, or absolute Love, was bestowed upon him. Returning to his homeland when he was thirty years old, the Christ Jesus opened the door for all men to enter the kingdom of heaven. He opened the door by showing them what was possible. Yet only if they believed that what he showed them was possible, was it

THE ORIGINS OF REIKI

possible. This power of belief became a cornerstone of his ministry. Over time he showed unequivocally that one of the most important factors in allowing the life force to fully express itself, and therefore heal, was through belief. You see, the life force is in every cell of our body, in the air we breathe, in the food we eat, and so on. Yet our own beliefs, if not aligned with the truth of our being, can block the life force from fully expressing. Time and time again this is pointed out by the Great Master. "Believe ye that I am able to do this?" Then, "According to your belief it is done unto you."[11]

Many more examples are given throughout the New Testament. Should you like to explore the power of these words, some of my favorite verses are Matthew 8:5 through 8:17, Matthew 9:20 though 9:22, Matthew 21:21 and 22, Mark 5:36 though 5:48 and John 11:14 and 15, 20 through 27 and 38 through 44. In First Timothy 4:10 through 4:15 we are encouraged to be examples of believers and use "the gift that is given us," the laying on of hands. Probably no other place in the Bible is this as apparent as when Jesus visited his home town of Nazareth after becoming The Christ. The people there remembered him only as a neighbor, the child of Joseph and Mary. "Is this not the brother of James, and Joses and of Juda and Simon? Are not his sisters here with us? And they were offended at him."[12] They just could not conceive that this neighborhood boy, now a man, could speak with such power and authority. "Who does he think he is?" was the energy behind their ridicule.

"And he could do there no mighty work; save that he laid his hands on a few sick folk and healed them. And he marveled because of their unbelief."[13]

You may ask yourself why he was able to heal through the laying on of hands when no other healing could be accomplished. The answer

---

11   Matthew 9:28-29, King James version – Scofield Reference Bible
12   Mark 6:3 – King James version – Scofield Reference Bible
13   Mark 6:5 – King James version – Scofield Reference Bible

THE NATURE OF REIKI: A PATH OF INCLUSION

is that people believed in the laying on of hands. It was part of the acceptable doctrine of their religion. But that was the extent of it. Likewise, in the traditional approach of working with Reiki, the laying on of hands is given priority for the same reasons. While it may be a stretch for some people, at least they've been exposed to it enough that it seems possible. "Miracles" on the other hand, are not likely to occur unless the power of influence which you carry with you can open a space for their possibility to exist.

We can begin to see then, that belief plays an important and fundamental role in allowing the "word of God" to wash through our being and heal our life. But what does healing really mean? Usually when people refer to healing they are talking about eliminating the symptoms of an illness or curing the disease itself. This is not necessarily healing. For unless there is a vibrational adjustment in thought or feelings, the illness will likely manifest again. Maybe not in the exact same place or way, but it probably will come back. When it does, and if this illness means the end of your life, does that mean that you cannot be healed? The answer is no. Even if you are on your death bed you can open to the healing balm of God and make your transition in peace. It is my belief that the greatest healing of all is peace.

A personal example of such healing came when my mother was dying of cancer. All of her life she bought into the values of modern society and had done her best to live within the framework of these values. While she was a loving mother, the fragmented guidelines of her time stopped her short of feeling able to express herself and be who she truly was. This resulted in a withdrawal from life as she grew in years, and in my opinion, strangled her capacity to feel life's joy. Once she was able to integrate the initial fear around her diagnosis with cancer, a new woman began to emerge. Her courage, strength, and loving heart began to open again. One incident in particular stands out in my mind. Since her youth she had been deathly afraid

THE ORIGINS OF REIKI

of thunderstorms. Her experience of being caught outside in a severe storm had stayed with her all her life. My brother, sisters, and I would sometimes laugh when it got the least bit cloudy as we knew mom would not go out of the house. One particular night after she was bedridden with the disease, a strong storm moved through our area. Anxious to see her the next morning, I walked into her room expecting to see a frightened woman. Much to my delight, she was sitting up in her bed with a tranquil look on her face. The sun shone through her window illuminating the radiance I perceived around her. A gentle smile of gratitude appeared on her face and she said, "Did you hear the storm last night honey? Wasn't it beautiful?" Astounded and relieved, I knew that while her body was dying, she was beginning to live again. I dare say that Reiki treatments and prayer helped to open the space for her to move into a place of peace. This place, as stated earlier, is the greatest healing there is.

In a larger than life example, Jesus played out an extreme drama which showed the power and peace of being fully connected to God as the ultimate way to live.

Ask yourself, while on the cross was Jesus wounded in his heart? Was he wounded in his judgment? Was his soul wounded? Not likely. Though his body was in excruciating pain he needed no healing. At this hour of destiny he had transcended the physical pain to such a degree that he was in full alignment with his truth. And from an incomprehensible depth of compassion and peace he asked for the forgiveness of his persecutors. "Father, forgive them for they know not what they do."[14] These were the words of a man so fully healed that even crucifixion could not keep him from peace.

Each one of us will someday make the final transition from the body. That is a given. The question is, do you want to do it in peace or in fear? No pill, no technique or modality can save us. So when I use the

---

14   Luke 23:34 – King James version – Scofield Reference Bible

THE NATURE OF REIKI: A PATH OF INCLUSION

word healing, I refer not only to the possibility of physical homeostasis, but also and more importantly, to that place inside of us that is not wounded or suffering even if our body appears to be. But, how do we get to such a place and what role does Reiki play in that journey?

CHOICES

"Nothing is good or bad,
but thinking makes it so."
Shakespeare

Ultimately we each decide what place Reiki (light and Love in motion) will play in our life. We have choices. We can choose to ignore the knocking on the door of our heart, or we can choose to open it. Opening the door may mean becoming vulnerable for a while as we release the ancient wounds within us, but it is also a means to allowing the passage of Love itself to and from this chamber of infinite depth. Let's talk about the vulnerability first since that is what keeps most of us from opening the door. So often we hear phrases like; "Just let it go." or "Don't think about it." "Be in the present." While these statements may ultimately be the answer, it doesn't usually seem so easy. Most of us don't know how to be okay with what has happened to us, what we feel we have done to others or how to acknowledge our "not enough-ness" to just let it go. How do we find peace when there's been no peace, or very little, in our life?

The answer is by aligning ourselves with the truth of who we really are. Think of yourself as little self and Reiki Self. Little self is the imposter who wants you to think that he/she is all there really is.

THE NATURE OF REIKI: A PATH OF INCLUSION

It is caught up in identity. It is also a master of camouflage. It will be anything it needs to be so that it stays invisible. You can begin to identify it by noticing its trail. It uses words like should, shouldn't, always, and can't. If you look closely you'll see that there is almost always an energy of judgment behind these words. Judgment, while we all do it, is the ego's projection of righteousness in an attempt to feel good enough and stay hidden. It is oftentimes "the pot calling the kettle black"!

The variations of employing our judgment on another are endless. A simple feeling or statement like "You shouldn't be...!" or "How can you...?" may be judgments based in the belief that our way of understanding is the only way to understand. Sometimes we may find ourselves projecting our beliefs onto someone; convinced that we are helping them when in fact our advice is to make us feel better or right. Religions, while they have helped many, are famous for this. The tragic result of holding onto our "rightness" has caused more suffering on this planet than perhaps anything else.

The right thing for me may not be the right thing for you. Should I eat meat? Should I be a vegetarian? Should I stop using sugar? Should I own health insurance? Should my children receive vaccines? These questions and more can only be decided by you. If, for example, I truly believed that eating sugar was bad for me and I let someone talk me into placing it in my food, I might feel a little twinge somewhere in my body as I was about to take the first bite. That twinge is key. It is telling me that I have given my power away. I am accepting your truth and not mine. So how do you think this sweet dish is going to sit with me? A great question to ask yourself to see if you're in alignment with an idea or concept is: "How does that thought make me feel?"

When you are out of alignment with yourself you feel bad, uncomfortable, or uneasy. When you are in alignment with yourself you feel good. It's that simple. If for example, you are having issues with prosperity, pay attention to your internal dialogue. Statements,

CHOICES

feelings or implications that support the consciousness of lack will feel disempowering. They make you feel small and hopeless. You can choose to shift a thought like "I don't have enough" to something like I Am the abundance of All That Is". By contemplating the second statement you can come into alignment with an empowering realization of who you are, namely that who you really are is "All That Is". It always has enough because there is nothing outside itself. If this seems like a difficult thought transition, please refer to the chapter on "I AM Affirmations". It should help clarify any confusion.

There are many other "bad feeling" thoughts that disempower us in such subtle ways that we don't even recognize them at first. How many times have you heard yourself or someone else say something like "Boy, I can't stand this heat anymore. It would be a nice day if we just had some cloud cover"? Truth is, you can and you are "standing the heat". It's just that you've created a story telling yourself you can't. Perhaps by simply acknowledging that it's hot outside you could experience the heat in a whole new way. Could it be just an experience? When you tell yourself "can't", you begin creating a self defeating program that eventually weakens your ability to cope with the world around you. In this case, when it's hot outside you automatically feel bad.

If you really want to live in a peaceful world, start by knowing that peace, like heaven, is within. The world according to societal norms and mass consciousness will never bring harmony into your life. It's up to you and you alone to uncover the beautiful garden of inner peace that lies beneath the jungle of overgrown thoughts.

Contemplate these examples for a little while and see if you can identify with their essence. In the first example, "enough" could refer to something other than money. After all, prosperity can be about many different components of life. In the second example it's easy enough to interchange the heat with countless examples of everyday things we

THE NATURE OF REIKI: A PATH OF INCLUSION

complain about. Could be the cold. Could be the humidity. Could be the driver in front of you.

Start making a list of the things "out there" that annoy you and bring an unsettling feeling to you when you think of them. Releasing these judgmental thoughts and energies will make the process of alignment with your Reiki Self much easier.

The following two exercises can be quite effective for releasing that old energy. Try them both and see which one feels right for you.

EXERCISE #1

When a thought gets stuck in your head there is usually a feeling from that thought that gets stuck in your body too. So close your eyes, think the thought, and locate the place in your body that feels uncomfortable when you think the thought. Now, imagine a door on the front and back of that area. Open the doors to create the effect of cross-ventilation and feel the fresh and vibrant life force energy moving through the area like a gentle wind. If you can visualize, you may notice that the stuck energy, which is now being gently dislodged, appears like gray or dark clouds as it moves out of the body.

At first this may seem difficult, especially if the pain has consumed you. But stop for a minute and notice. Is the wind still blowing? Are the birds still singing? Are the ocean waves still coming ashore in their endless cycle of motion? Is the earth still spinning and my body still breathing? If you answer yes to any of those questions then you know that Life is still in motion, and that you, as an inseparable part of life, must also be in motion. Feel that peaceful flow of energy entering into your body through the open doors. Allow it to revitalize the area as it relaxes and renews the damaged tissue. Feel the area becoming lighter until all the dark clouds are gone and peace returns. Even if you are only successful at feeling this peace for

CHOICES

a moment you have created a crack in the wall of your reality. That's how the light gets in. Repeat as needed, feeling the crack become larger and larger until finally the reality of light and Love has established itself again. Each time you are able to shift your vibration from darkness to light you begin to attract more positive things into your life. Eventually this will completely turn your life around.

EXERCISE #2

Another energy feeling exercise that can help is to close your eyes and imagine a large ball of radiant light in front of you. Feel the warmth of its glow. As your inner vision begins to adjust to its radiance, notice its brilliance growing more and more intense in each passing moment. Finally, the light is so bright that you can no longer look upon it. It seems like the sun. Your entire being is surrounded by its loving warmth; nurturing you to the depth of your soul.

From this space of loving warmth you begin to feel your muscles relax and the tension drain away from your body. Now, pull this radiant ball of light into your body and feel it disintegrate the energy blocks you are holding within. Watch it vaporize any darkness or heavy feelings that you sense may be inside of you. When no more darkness or heavy feelings remain, notice that the radiance of this light is beginning to fill each and every cell of your body until your entire being is glowing with the sweetness of life.

These exercises can clear the way for making choices that are in alignment with who you are in this moment. After working with them you can continue to align with your Reiki Self by meditating or contemplating an "I AM" affirmation (see the Chapter on Affirmations) or any other affirmation that may be helpful. You could also go for a

THE NATURE OF REIKI: A PATH OF INCLUSION

walk in nature, receive a Reiki treatment, or anything that helps you sense your unbounded Self.

Knowing how Reiki may have been used in the past can ignite our imagination and help us understand the potential in our present time, which we have only begun to explore. This current exploration must include, if it's to be of lasting value, an honest look at what most of us don't want to look at… our dark side.

EMBRACING OUR DARK SIDE

*"When we deny the parts of ourselves that we feel are unacceptable –
we deny the wholeness of who we are."*
John David Sparks

Each of us has a dark side. Most of us spend our entire life trying to hide or deny that side of ourselves. In the world of Reiki, the world of light and Love, we may feel that there is no place for this part of ourselves to exist. We could not be farther from the truth.

If it were not for the darkness, would we be able to see the light? They are married, like all opposites on this planet are. When we look into the night sky, why do you suppose we can see the endless array of stars and planets that exist? You guessed it. Because of the darkness. And so it is with all things existing in this three dimensional reality, even within ourselves.

When we deny the parts of ourselves that we feel are unacceptable - the dark parts - we deny the wholeness of who we are. And just because we acknowledge our dark side, it doesn't diminish our light. In fact it expands us. Life becomes so much simpler when we can acknowledge all the parts of our self that no one wants to claim. The reality that we all share the same issues, stresses, problems and so called flaws is something we rarely acknowledge. We would rather project our undesirable traits

THE NATURE OF REIKI: A PATH OF INCLUSION

onto someone else so that we don't have to look bad. However, when we acknowledge all of ourselves it frees up tremendous energy to focus on that which we wish to experience instead of hiding from that which we don't. If, for example, someone tells me I'm arrogant and I've spent my life trying to be humble, I might easily go into defense around my humbleness. Oddly enough, that defense now brings out my arrogance. Wouldn't it be easier to simply know and own that part of me which has inspired my humbleness... my arrogance? So instead of defending myself I could simply say, "Yes, I have found that part of me too. I'm trying to focus on humility but I can see that it doesn't always come through. Sorry if I offended you." In this way I don't have to try and maintain an impossible standard for myself. I express genuineness, compassion, humility, and connect to the world instead of disconnecting. By that I mean that as soon as I go on the defense, the person I'm responding to goes on defense and walls of isolation are created. Even if we remain friends on the outside, unless the truth is acknowledged there will begin to be small resentments adding up to a potentially volatile climax. Then it is usually too late.

Practice acknowledging and owning all the traits that trigger you. As you read the following list of words, try to imagine – – really imagine – – that a newspaper article is being written about you using one or more of these words. Write down the ones that trigger a negative emotional response and see if you can find that quality in yourself. It could be a trait that is currently in your life or one you feel is from your past. Some of the more common examples are: worthless, stupid, gullible, vain, phony, arrogant, deceitful, ugly, unfair, slow, demanding, manipulating, aloof, controlling, stubborn, liar, lazy, shallow, beautiful, generous, perfect, balanced, nice, good looking, cute, intelligent, talented, spiritual.

By acknowledging and owning all aspects of our self, we can begin to break free of the chains of duality. A new path begins to emerge, one which exists beyond good and bad; one that sees oneness. A path that

EMBRACING OUR DARK SIDE

carries us beyond all judgment and back to our home within the heart of God where the essence of who we are exists beyond thought. This home vibrates as pure consciousness imbued with life force. It is this life, the Reiki life, which has expressed itself individually through each of us. As you go through the list you may find yourself acknowledging part of your dark side that has control over you. For example, let's say you've acknowledged and finally accepted that you manipulate people for your own gain. You feel pretty lousy about yourself because you can remember some not so nice outcomes. Maybe you feel you really hurt someone by your selfish acts. Maybe you recognized this trait a long time ago but justified your actions instead of simply looking at the truth. Now the gig is up, but you don't know how to change. You've tried before but it appears that you are so afraid of not getting what you want that you continue the same pattern of behavior. What do you do?

Try to do nothing. That's right, do nothing. Just accept the aspect or aspects of yourself you have been afraid to look at and stop the struggle of denial. Sit with it. Acknowledge it, and acknowledge the fear, the guilt, the sadness, or whatever impact it has had on you and do your best to stay away from judgment. This may be incredibly difficult, but understand that accepting does not mean condoning. Just observe. For example, when you look at the night sky do you judge the darkness? No. You simply acknowledge that it provides the depth and backdrop for observing the light of an incredible, never ending universe. The darkness and the light co-exist in harmony and you can too. Your personal darkness can be the gift of bringing your focus to your light if you will allow it. "Be" who you are - you are nothing less than the son/daughter of "All That Is". The more acquainted you "be"come with yourself, the more you'll discover that you've already got what you're looking for.

Remember, in order for a so-called negative trait to exist, the opposite also has to be present. It is then a matter of focusing your attention on that part of you which you wish to express. It's not "out there". It's already inside of you.

An old Indian story called Two Wolves illustrates this beautifully.

TWO WOLVES

One evening an old Cherokee told his grandson about a
battle that goes on inside people. He said, "My son, the
battle is between two 'wolves' inside us all.
One is Evil. It is anger, envy, jealousy, sorrow, regret, greed,
arrogance, self-pity, guilt, resentment, inferiority, lies, false
pride, superiority, and ego.
The other is Good. It is joy, hope, kindness, determination,
optimism, love, empathy, generosity, truth, compassion, and
cooperation."
The grandson thought about it for a minute and then asked
his grandfather "Which wolf wins?"
The old Cherokee simply replied, "The one you feed."

Turn to the "I AM" affirmations section of the book and feed yourself with the truth that lives in them. Remember the truth of who you are. The I AM, is the life force (The Reiki energy) turned all the way up. In reality, it exists beyond the duality we live in, yet it encompasses all of it.

By seeing and accepting that we are all of it, we empower ourselves with the ability to choose. On the contrary, by focusing all of our attention on who or what we don't want to be, we stay in the prison of that identity box. Abraham, as channeled by Esther Hicks, once said, "You limit yourself only by your attention to what you don't want." So there is really nothing to do, only behavior to observe. Without judgment. And from that place of acceptance you can simply choose which aspects of yourself you want to experience.

EMBRACING OUR DARK SIDE

Make friends with your dark side, or shadow self as it is sometimes called. It has served you in many ways. As you review the list of qualities that trigger you, try to understand how these qualities have also helped move you to the perfect time and place for true change to occur, right now. It is only our belief that we should have been, or must now be, a certain way which creates the barrier of self acceptance. And while this barrier likely goes back to the beginning of our time as humans, it can still be of value today to take a look at shifting some of our current beliefs.

BELIEFS

"Truth stands alone;
it doesn't need your belief to give it reality."
Michael Misita

Beliefs are thoughts and feelings we hold as true about ourselves and the world around us. Many beliefs are anchored in our minds when we are very young, perhaps even before we learn to speak. Some of these beliefs are very empowering and some very disempowering. Once they are anchored, these beliefs send out a signal, or vibration, about who we are. Or, more appropriately stated, who we believe we are. The law of "likes attract" then begins to draw to us situations and people that match our beliefs thus confirming that they (our beliefs) must be true. This process can become one of the greatest obstacles or greatest blessings in our life. The question is "What do we believe?" And in this context, how does what we believe impact Reiki?

Given that belief is one of the most powerful forces on the planet, it would be wise to align our beliefs and our Reiki awareness together. After all, we're talking about the unlimited possibilities of vibrating with a larger and larger spectrum of Life energy which will then draw to us larger and larger possibilities of union with the Divine. This will not only impact our own awareness, but also create an aura of influence to

THE NATURE OF REIKI: A PATH OF INCLUSION

those who come to us for healing. Immediately your client will know on an energetic level whether they are in the presence of someone who is in their heart and "knows", or in their head and "thinks they know".

While it's true that Reiki doesn't depend on a particular belief system to work, it is also true that our beliefs can allow and even amplify the effectiveness of Reiki. Let's face it, we're alive. If we're alive then the life force energy must be operating within us. It doesn't need our belief to bring life to the body. Yet, by dwelling on negative thoughts, which include fear, we can greatly diminish the flow of healthy life energy to all or part of the body. If not corrected, this can cause pain, depression, and even disease.

So first we must work on ourselves to instill the truth of unlimited possibilities that flow through us. Then we can assist those around us who come for healing. Two very effective ways to do this is through affirmations and meditation. Affirmations, if deeply felt, are like doors to greater possibilities. They are not the truth but doorways to the truth. Meditation can help us through the doorway and become the vehicle through which new awareness is made possible.

As greater awareness is anchored into our vibration, our expanding knowledge allows a space for our client's beliefs to expand. This then will give us the backdrop for a more effective healing. Who among us is not influenced when we read or hear the testimonial of someone who has been healed? The more testimonials we know of, the more open we become.

Going back again to the stories of Jesus we find powerful examples of how his fame was ignited through those who believed. Take a look at some of the Bible passages that bear witness to this power. Matthew 9:18 through 9:31 recount three miraculous healings in just one story. First there is the story of the lady who touched Jesus' robe while he was on his way to help a woman who was presumed dead. As she did so, he turned to her and said "Daughter, be of good comfort, thy faith hath

BELIEFS

made thee whole". When he arrived at his destination, the presumed dead woman was brought back to wholeness. After this incident, his fame spread far, fostering even greater belief among the people. As he was departing, two blind men asked him to restore their sight at which he replied "Believe ye that I am able to do this?" When they answered yes he touched their eyes saying "According to your faith be it unto you". They departed spreading his fame even more.

These stories inspire us and help us to see how important it is to align our beliefs with greater truths. Other passages you may find of interest are Mark 8:22-26, John 14:12 and Matthew 21:21-22. In the first story Jesus heals a blind man by first leading him out of town away from people. Then after the healing says to him "Neither go into the town nor tell it to any in the town". This was because the man's faith was not solid. If he listened to the many doubters around town who would tell him what happened was impossible or perhaps that it was even the work of the devil, his belief would have wavered and his blindness return. This is an important lesson to us all. Let the doubters doubt. Allow them to live in their world of limitation, but if their power of influence causes you to live in their world, it's better to go "out of town" or just not talk with them at all.

The second reference to John 14:12 is simply about our ability through belief. Jesus says "Verily, verily I say unto you, he that believeth in me, the works I do shall he do also". Remember, Jesus was the Christ. He had lost his identity to become the absolute Love, which is the only "son" or offspring of God. Try not to get confused about what he is asking us to believe in.

Finally, in Matthew 12:21-22 Jesus states with perhaps his greatest clarity "If ye have faith and doubt not, ye shall not only do this which is done to the fig tree, but also if ye shall say unto this mountain, be thou removed and be thou cast into the sea; it shall be done. And all things, whatsoever ye shall ask in prayer, believing, ye shall receive".

THE NATURE OF REIKI: A PATH OF INCLUSION

Another one of my favorite stories is Matthew 8:5-17. I like this one so much because it demonstrates how belief becomes a pathway for distance healing. In it, a centurion comes to Jesus with a request for healing his servant. When Jesus replied by saying he would come and heal him, the centurion answered "Lord, I am not worthy that thou should come under my roof: but speak the word only and my servant shall be healed." In verse 13 Jesus sums up his awe at this man's belief by saying "Go thy way; and as thou hast believed, so be it done unto thee."

As you can see, the Bible is full of stories which inspire us to reach for our greatest potential through believing, but it's not the only book that acknowledges its power. In the classic "Autobiography of a Yogi" by Paramahansa Yogananda, Sri Yukteswar, Yogananda's Guru, relates an incredible story of how belief helped him gain fifty pounds in one day after a severe illness. The story is so inspiring that it is read as part of our Reiki Master Training Course. You probably have a few books in your own library that have expanded the limits of your consciousness through the power of belief.

Could we really get where we want to go by doubting?

Now, for someone to come to a Reiki practitioner there must already be a certain amount of belief in place. Our work then, is to move into a deep place of belief, and ultimately knowledge within one self which allows our client to open even further. We must see our client as whole, not broken, sense the truth behind the screen of visible evidence that they are unwell, and become grounded in the awareness that wholeness is our true nature. No matter how ill someone may appear to be, it is only an appearance. The body may be riddled with disease but the truth of who we are lies beyond a diseased body. Allow your belief to lead you to this understanding and then tap into that truth and stay there for the length of your session. Allow the Reiki to flow through our open channels of alignment and leave the rest to God.

BELIEFS

The importance of understanding Reiki in the broad perspective offered throughout these pages lies in the unlimited potential for Self awareness and Divine guidance not generally recognized when we approach Reiki as something we "*do*". It is rather something we "*are*". From this perspective we can begin to unfold into the limitless nature of Self and tap into a greater understanding of Oneness. Here, on this path is where I believe Reiki holds its greatest treasure. Without an understanding of who we are, peace, happiness, and all the things we long for to make our life better will continue to evade us.

Along with the concepts and considerations already stated, there are tools that can help us open our minds and anchor a new energy of understanding in our lives. One such tool is affirmations, particularly I AM affirmations.

AFFIRMATIONS

*"When we understand that most, if not all, of our thoughts
are simply a single function of Mind, we begin to realize
that who we are exists beyond thought."*
John David Sparks

Affirmations can be used along with oils, stones, color, herbs, or by themselves. With the proper intention and alignment, they can become the verbal vibration of Reiki; the word of God. Jesus said, "Man shall not live by bread alone, but by every word that proceedeth out of the mouth of God."[15] Words of true conviction, faith, sincerity and intention are highly explosive vibrational bombs that resonate in our bodies, altering the vibrational tone of every cell. It has been my observation that a Reiki treatment assisted by affirmations (or vice versa) will increase the focus and potency of the treatment. Part of the reason this is so is because an affirmation spoken with true conviction reflects the belief of you and/or your client. Do not underestimate the power of belief. Remember, energy follows thought. Your thought reflects your beliefs. Even though there is truth beyond belief, it is perhaps the most powerful tool you have to lead you to it. USE IT!!! Water the truth of your words with showers of Reiki. By allowing

---

15   Matthew 4:4 – King James version – Scofield Reference Bible

THE NATURE OF REIKI: A PATH OF INCLUSION

the Reiki energy to impregnate your words with light and Love, they become atomic bombs. If, however, they are not empowered with Spirit, they are, as Paramahansa Yogananda says, like husks without corn. Every affirmation you use should be deeply felt as true. Many people have difficulty with this concept because they cannot see past the illness or situation as it has been. It is therefore important to remember two things. One, that the past is the past. Eckhart Tolle, in his book "A New Earth" states "There is nothing that has ever happened in the past that can stop you from being present now." Now doesn't mean the future, it means <u>now</u>. Ponder the possibilities of this statement and become like the disciple Paul who proclaimed "I die daily."[16] Most of us have been missing the present moment by thinking about the past and projecting it into the future. We can shift that behavior simply by observing - not judging - our thoughts in action. When we understand that most, if not all, of our thoughts are simply a single function of Mind, we begin to realize that who we are exists beyond thought. Therefore we exist beyond the past, we exist right here and now. This awareness aligns us with the light and Love that Reiki is; the light and Love that is always flowing, ever changing, never changing, and eternally Now.

The second thing we can do is look past the obvious. For example, if you are a smoker and you want to quit smoking, ask yourself who is smoking. If you are attached to your identity as a smoker this will be difficult. But, if you look deeper and maybe ask yourself a few questions, you can loosen the grip of your identity. Were you a smoker when you were born? Will you be a smoker after you die? Who or what is really smoking? Quickly you'll discern that the flesh and blood you've always called you, along with a pattern of developed neurosis, is responsible for the cigarette occupying your time. The "You" of you is not a smoker. It simply observes this habit the body has acquired. The You of you came

---

16   Corinthians 15:31 – King James version – Scofield Reference Bible

AFFIRMATIONS

into this world without a smoke, and once separated from the body, will again be smoke free.

Take a moment or two and tap into that truth before you begin your affirmation. The essence of You is not a smoker. You are a spark of Divinity experiencing itself in matter. In fact, the concept and experience of yourself as a spark of divinity is the most important concept you can embrace for demonstrating your affirmation in the material world. In the Usui system of Reiki, the master symbol (which we'll get to later) is all about claiming this spark of Divinity as who you are. The Bible states this premise right from the beginning. Genesis 1:26-27 state that man is created in the likeness and the image of God. "When Moses spoke to God through the burning bush and asked God his name, God replied, "I AM that I AM. Say unto the children of Israel I AM hath sent me unto you."[17] God had told Moses that his/her name is I AM. It is interesting to note that the word "name" is sometimes translated meaning "nature." Thus, I AM describes the Nature of God as the core and essence within each human being. The "sound" of God's name is best described by Jonathan Goldman in his book "The Divine Name." For our purposes, the name (or nature) of God as that I AM, is sufficient for our affirmations. For who can say "I AM" except each and every person for themselves?

So when you state an affirmation prefaced with I AM, identify not with the flesh and blood you see in the mirror, but with the spark of divinity that gives it life: that I AM! In time you will begin to feel a greater sense of humility and awe as you realize that of yourself, you do nothing. Who *you* are is so beyond the concepts of mind you will be brought to your knees in humble acknowledgment of this truth. Ego has very little or no place in this awareness.

If you know the Usui Master Symbol, activate the symbol before you begin, as some of the most powerful affirmations you can state are

---

17   Exodus 3:14 – King James version – Scofield Reference Bible

THE NATURE OF REIKI: A PATH OF INCLUSION

the I AM Affirmations. I AM is pure consciousness expressing itself through you. It is your choice to demonstrate the aspect of divinity you wish to experience. And, since the qualities of God that we are focusing on are designed to offer us a more balanced view of ourselves, it is important to go deep into each aspect. These aspects are Life, Light, Love, Peace, Power, Beauty, Joy, Balance, Abundance, Health, and Dynamic Stability. As each aspect is highlighted through your affirmation, stop and consider the full scope of that aspect. For example, if you are choosing to experience peace, ponder the many expressions of peace that are all around you.

> Stop and feel the peace that is so present during sunrise or sunset.
>
> Stop and feel the peace that is felt through the sound of ocean waves.
>
> Stop and feel the peace we have in existing friendships.
>
> Stop and feel the peace we feel during prayer or meditation.
>
> Stop and feel the peace we sense as we walk through nature.

Then recognize that these expressions of peace are expressions of I AM, or God. Now, place the name of God, I AM, in front of those expressions and you will see that there is no way to separate you from peace. You will, over time, begin to recognize and identify yourself as that aspect, in this case peace.

> I AM the peace that is present during sunrise or sunset.
>
> I AM the peace that is felt through the sound of ocean waves.

AFFIRMATIONS

I AM the peace within friendships.

I AM the peace that is felt during prayer and meditation.

I AM the peace that is felt as I walk through nature.

In each situation feel yourself as the omnipresent quality of God that you are presently claiming. How else could you know the feeling of peace (in this case) if it weren't already a part of who you are?

The following are examples of affirmations that may be helpful in treatment for yourself or another. They are broken up into general categories for your convenience. Say them slowly giving thought to each phrase. If questions or other thoughts arise as you embrace them, write them down. Deep inquiry into the truth of their nature will serve you well. In this way, your own affirmations will come forth easily and your understanding will be greater. You will find that some of the affirmations start with acknowledging the "little I" before aligning with the unlimited "I". If you find one you don't resonate with at all, simply move on.

AFFIRMATIONS FOR PHYSICAL HEALING (GENERAL OVERVIEW)

I AM the source of balance and health throughout all creation.

The grace and beauty I AM melts away the dis-ease in my life and restores me to balance.

Pause here. If you are having difficulty acknowledging the beauty you are, or any aspect of Source that you are, stop and write down where in your life you feel or have felt beautiful (or whatever aspect you're having difficulty with). Perhaps it was when you played with your children. Perhaps it was when you went to your high school prom. Perhaps it was when you were making love. Or perhaps it was

55

THE NATURE OF REIKI: A PATH OF INCLUSION

just when you had a kind thought about someone or something. Simply acknowledging the beauty in someone or something else reflects the beauty you are. How else could you recognize it?

Once you discover that you already are the aspect of God in question, claiming "I AM" that aspect becomes much easier.

If all else fails in shifting your perception of who you are, simply claim the I AM as God. Remember, it is his/her name. In the example of beauty it would be like saying the beauty that God is. But since God's name is I AM you say "The beauty I AM".

As you can see, there is no way to separate the You of you from God. Every time you say I AM you are acknowledging yourself as a divine spark of the creator. So let's continue.

> *I acknowledge and embrace the Living expression of radiant health I AM.*
>
> *I AM the consciousness of perfect health that permeates my body.*
>
> *The presence of God within me is expressing the nature of vibrant vitality I AM.*
>
> *I acknowledge, honor and align myself with the consciousness and feeling of the vibrant health I AM.*
>
> *I AM vibrant health and vitality expressing through form and individualized as me: _____ (Insert your name) _____ .*

AFFIRMATIONS FOR FEAR OF CHANGE

Fear of change can negatively impact, and create imbalances relative to, the bladder, bowels, morning sickness, chronic diseases, constipation, diarrhea, joints, foot problems, heartburn, hip problems, indigestion,

AFFIRMATIONS

insomnia, leg problems, miscarriage, nausea, sterility, ulcers, and more.

> *The Father within, that I AM, leads me safely to the still waters of my soul.*
>
> *I AM the stillness within the winds of change.*
>
> *I AM the natural and healthy flow of Life's desire to change.*
>
> *I AM the way of courage, hope, and ever expanding faith in life's journey toward its highest expression.*
>
> *I AM the living expression of ever expanding awareness that flows effortlessly throughout the universe.*
>
> *I AM the rich omnipresent substance of the universe through which all things find balance.*
>
> *I acknowledge, embrace and align myself with the consciousness and feeling that I AM safe through all of life's changes.*

AFFIRMATIONS FOR LOVE

Undoubtedly the largest four letter word in the English language, love, has been spindled, folded, twisted and mutilated more than any other state of being on earth. Why? Because it's way too vast to fit inside our little conceptual boxes of how it should act, how it should look, what it should feel like, and with whom and how it should be shared. Trying to control Love is a folly. The joy, the peace, and the presence of Love are interchangeable concepts with God. The problem with words and concepts are that we often mistake them as the thing itself. Our concept of Love is just that, a concept. Trying to describe Love is like the finger that points to the path. We will never walk the path if we continue to focus on the finger.

THE NATURE OF REIKI: A PATH OF INCLUSION

In using the affirmations about love, try to drop your concepts of love and align your thoughts and feelings with the Love of God. This Love knows no bounds. It graciously accepts and embraces everybody's path as perfect. No exceptions. Just because we can't understand a situation in the moment doesn't mean that it isn't perfect. In fact, what else could it be? I'm reminded of a story about George the Priest. One evening after George had watched the news he became very upset. For too long now he had read and heard of the escalating violence in his area and in the world. Enough was enough. He felt helpless and saddened that so much violence was in the heart of his fellow man. So he decided that he was going to pray unceasingly to God to help save the world. He vowed not to stop until he heard the voice of God telling him what to do. Immediately he began his prayers. For hours he petitioned God to talk to him, to ease his pain, and tell him what to do. All through the night he prayed and into the next day. Occasionally the intensity of his request reached such a crescendo that he thought he would collapse. Then, finally, on the second night George heard the voice of God. It said "George, you can go to sleep now, I'll take over".

Our belief that the world should be different than it is can become our road to self torture. On the other hand, accepting it as it is can bring about the perfect opportunity to express our heart and create the change we so deeply desire. The first path argues with reality. We can become consumed in our argument and never really change anything. This only leads to more stress and discontent in our life. The second path sees clearly what is, and rather than argue with it, simply acknowledges whether or not the heart is engaged sufficiently to pursue a compassionate course of action. The first way is of the mind, the second way is of the heart. This is the Reiki path, the path of the heart.

Affirmations around love should be loving and compassionate. They should allow for everyone and everything, including yourself.

AFFIRMATIONS

Understand that we are all exactly where we are supposed to be, doing exactly what we are supposed to do given the knowledge and events in our life up to this time. After all, love, or should I say the lack of it, can impact our body/mind in a myriad of ways. This could include general body ache, addictions, adrenal problems, anxiety, upper back problems, blood problems, liver disorders, pancreatitis, thymus problems, ulcers, and more. Basically stated, love brings the feeling of empowerment. If you are feeling disempowered by a person or situation, try adding love to the formula.

> *I allow the beauty of God's Love, the Love I AM, to guide me to the next right step in my healing.*
>
> *I allow the beauty and power of God's Love to be recognized as the beauty and power I AM.*
>
> *I Love and approve of myself just the way I am, for the journey of my errors has brought me to this perfect place of starting new.*
>
> *I Love those who I feel have wronged me. For through them my boundaries of Love have a chance to expand.*
>
> *I am open, willing, and ready to receive the Love I AM.*
>
> *The Love I AM magnetizes my being and draws to me those to share my Love with.*
>
> *I AM unconditional Love, expressing through form and individualized as me, _____(Insert your name)_____, drawing the perfect circumstances and people into my life to share this unlimited joy.*

AFFIRMATIONS FOR LOSS AND GRIEF

Grief is a natural process that should be honored and not shoved in a box. "Big boys don't cry", "get over it and move on", and more,

THE NATURE OF REIKI: A PATH OF INCLUSION

are statements that, if allowed, could repress this natural expression of love.

First affecting the heart, deep sorrow and grief can spread quickly, impacting every part of the body/mind and isolating us from the truth of our connectedness and joy from which the sorrow sprang.

The key to honoring grief in a healthy way is to always remain aware that emotions are not who we are. They are expressions of response to deep connections and ideas we have about the world.

The following affirmations are based in the understanding of ourselves as creatures of God with a deep capacity for expressing love. May you find peace within them.

I AM the all pervading spirit of Universal Love. My loss brings me to see the depth and timeless nature of Life.

The wound in my heart has created a crack for the light to come in. I feel the light, I feel the Love, I AM the light, I AM the Love.

Deep beneath tumultuous waves, the serene realization of that I AM remains the stable truth.

The eternal tides of life wash the shores of my experience with wonder, with awe, and with understanding that life, while ever changing, is never ending.

The Universal Light and Love that I AM, clears all thoughts of separation and keeps my heart in union with my beloved.

The turbulent waves of grief that rise are carried to the shores of stability and understanding by the current of omnipresent Love I AM.

The loss I feel shallows in comparison to the eternal Love from which it sprang.

AFFIRMATIONS FOR ABUNDANCE

Abundance is the opposite of lack. Lack means a restricted flow. Abundance means an open flow. Restrictions in the body/mind are simply the inability to allow the unrestricted flow of life force into your being. It is usually associated with the thought of money although such a thought is restricting in itself. When you open to the abundance in your life, not only will money begin to flow, but your entire life will begin to change. Relationships, synchronicities, and even tight, restricted areas of the body will begin to heal. Some of the most common restrictions manifest in the body through abdominal cramps, alcoholism, anemia, anxiety, apathy, appendicitis, back problems, Bell's palsy, blood problems, bowel problems, breathing problems, bursitis, cold sores, fatigue, gland problems, heart problems, heartburn, joint problems, impotence, some psychiatric illnesses, lockjaw, nervousness, spasms, stiffness, and more.

Once again, by using the I AM affirmations, the restricting beliefs of ego can be overshadowed by a greater truth. Feel these truths deep inside of you and recognize yourself as an integral part of the flow of life. Feel yourself as worthy because you are! Worthiness is a struggle for many people because self judgment gets in the way. You may find yourself saying "No, I'm not judging myself, but my neighbor is always talking about me. She's the one judging." Now, this may be a fact, but it's not the truth. Unless you accept such a judgment it will not restrict the flow of abundance in your life, but when you do, the judgment *will* restrict the flow. If and when you accept such judgment it becomes self judgment. If this has happened to you or if you are in a constant state of negative comparison, you need to forgive yourself. Rest assured that God is not judging you. God has given us free will so that we can learn what feels right; what feels compassionately empowering in our lives. Most often this is discovered by first experiencing what we don't want. It's the nature of the dualistic world we live in. What God would give

THE NATURE OF REIKI: A PATH OF INCLUSION

us such choices and then condemn us for choosing them? So worthiness is not a word in Gods dictionary. We simply are. We are aspects of The Divine, picking and choosing the experiences in our life that bring us into alignment with that truth. The sun shines on every face whether ignorant, wounded, or wise. When that truth becomes your belief, take one more step and watch your dominant vibration shift to begin attracting abundance in all ways. Use these affirmations to help.

> *I gratefully acknowledge and express the infinite abundance I AM.*
>
> *I lovingly acknowledge the self worth that I AM (Note: you cannot accept God's abundance if you do not feel you are worth it.)*
>
> *I AM the living expression of infinite prosperity and abundance.*
>
> *I AM lavish abundance expressing through form and individualized as me, _____(Insert your name)_____, through whom the idea of money finds fertile soil to grow and demonstrate itself in ever expanding and joyous ways.*
>
> *Beyond the limits of conscious mind, beyond the world of thought, the ever expanding light and Love of God I AM draws to me the perfect circumstances and people, creating financial abundance and a balanced life.*
>
> *The abundance God is, I AM.*
>
> *I am open, willing, and ready to receive the abundance of that I AM.*

AFFIRMATION FOR SELF WORTH

On a personal note regarding my Reiki path, I have needed to see the full spectrum of self worth that I AM. To do this I have lived the down of it and the up of it; the bad of it and the good of it. I have played with

AFFIRMATIONS

the feeling of worthlessness long enough to see it is rooted in the concept of worthiness which I must also understand on some level to play this game. In reality, both are just stories in my mind. From now on I choose the story that makes me feel good. For in truth, God is --- I AM. Of all God's expressions, man is the only one who struggles with the issue of self worth. Our reasoning mind would have us believe that it is possible to be unworthy. This is the mind of judgment of which God has no part, except in allowing this duality to exist for our evolution. "Judge not lest ye be judged"[18] are the words Jesus used to help us understand that judgment is of the little self. When we identify with the little self we are in the world of judgment. When we are "being", we are in the world of the God Self where judgment does not exist. When we judge another we can expect to be judged because that is the vibrational world we are resonating with. In opening to the expansiveness of Reiki, we come to know ourselves as a part of the great web of life. No one part can exist without the other. Therefore self worth issues cease to exist. ALL are worthy.

> *I AM pure consciousness expressing through form and individualized as me, _____(Insert your name)_____, in whom self worth is recognized and made manifest.*
>
> *The presence of that I AM exists beyond the judgment of self worth. The presence of that I AM - IS.*
>
> *I AM the consciousness of Love that expresses without judgment.*
>
> *The light and Love of that I AM shines brightly for all, for all are worthy.*
>
> *Before language and beneath thought, the stillness of that I AM can find no judgment.*

---

18   Matthew 7:1 – King James version – Scofield Reference Bible

THE NATURE OF REIKI: A PATH OF INCLUSION

In opening to the expansiveness of that I AM, I recognize light because of darkness, strong because of weak, and joy because of sorrow – which is worth more?

Made in the image and likeness of the creator I AM self worth.

Hopefully you've already begun to sense the potential these affirmations hold in helping you understand yourself as a child of God.

Make your resolve now, dedicate yourself to the understanding that "I AM" is all that there is. Decide how you want to live your life and intend that every thought and action is leading you to your vision and beyond. In fact, becoming clear about your intention will bring your choices, your beliefs, and your ability to embrace all aspects of yourself into alignment. So let's look at intention a little deeper.

INTENTION

"All your client has really come for,
is to discover your Loving intent."
John David Sparks

In Reiki training the world of energy can become tangible very quickly, usually within hours or sometimes within minutes. Regardless of whether you're in a Reiki class or becoming attuned to the energy in some other way, intention of how to work with the energy is the next step.

As mentioned before, consciousness expansion and a hands-on-healing approach are the two most common ways. Most people start with the hands-on approach either with themselves or another. This seems to work really well since feedback is often involved. It gives you a chance to know objectively how the energy is working, so let's start there.

Keep in mind that the Universal Life Force is imbued with its own intelligence. Telling it what to do or how to act is not necessary. In fact, such directives could bolster the ego's belief that it is in control, and therein lies some words of caution. Most people involved in energy healing are working with a power beyond their comprehension. Trying

THE NATURE OF REIKI: A PATH OF INCLUSION

to manipulate the energy could create difficulties unless your intention in offering Reiki is <u>always</u> that the highest good be served.

This does not mean that directing Reiki to a specific illness should necessarily be avoided. The avoidance should be around playing God. If an illness is to be destroyed it will be, if it is not, then the energy will simply flow to the place where it is most needed. Let go of your attachment to a specific outcome! Healing occurs perfectly for each person according to Universal Laws, many of which are beyond our present scope of understanding. It's really out of our hands. All you can do, and all your client has really come for, is to discover your Loving intent. Reiki is the perfect vehicle for offering this Love.

When I stated that trying to manipulate the energy might create difficulties, I was referring to difficulties that the mind likes to create. For thousands of years man has allowed the thinking mind to dominate his/her behavior. The problem is that we have other components of our being which are equally important and have been stuffed away. This has created a great imbalance in the way we live. It's time to live in balance. The entire planet depends on it. The ego structure around most of humanity is built with walls of control. Those walls are so thick and so high that we have come to believe there is no other reality. By trying to manipulate the Reiki we are asking this energy from "beyond the beyond" to stay contained within the tiny box of our understanding. This is where the difficulty could come in. It's like saying that love can only extend to one person and that person should respond this way or that way to our love. The truth is, Love is boundless and impacts everybody in a unique way. By attempting to control the Reiki, it's easy to begin thinking of yourself as the healer. This view is a little misleading because a Reiki practitioner simply holds a loving space where the Innate intelligence of "All That is" does its work relative to the intention and capacity of the client. If the person you are working on is in alignment, that is, in acceptance

INTENTION

with their request for healing, the Reiki energy will act as a bridge connecting them with their desire. If they are not in alignment with their request for healing, the Reiki energy may help them get in alignment with that request.

As the Reiki energy flows through you, around you, and to a degree, mixes with the energy of your client, you become as one. The combination of providing a safe, loving environment where the client feels free to unfold, and the influx of vibrant life force energy, allows them to free themselves from the stubborn fear based patterns lodged in their system. You, as the practitioner, don't really "do" anything except hold the space and let the energy flow. Some people hear these words but continue to act as though *they* are the healer. Others fall into fear as they consider the ramifications of mixing energy with the clients. They fear they will take on the wounds or karma of the person they are working with.

Let's talk about that. When you are at a distance from another, setting up energetic barriers of protection around yourself can be done quite easily. Using the Reiki Power Symbol is one such way. As you go about your day, the protection it provides keeps you from picking up too much negative energy from others. But when you're offering Reiki in a one on one session you are intentionally opening a pathway for energy to be shared. It is simply a part of the process.

Reiki flows freely between you as your compassionate heart allows the healing process to take place. Under such circumstances it is possible to take on your client's wounds or karma. By karma I am referring to the consequence of the volition of an action or a thought. Often times these consequences lead to creating particular patterns in our life which serve as building blocks for our evolution. Good, bad, or otherwise, it doesn't matter. It's the energy of action, however subtle it may be. Good and bad are just concepts of the mind. The Reiki energy itself stays pure but the quality of energy it releases could be muddled in karma.

THE NATURE OF REIKI: A PATH OF INCLUSION

The good news is that it doesn't have to stay in your system long at all. It can pass through quickly if you stay out of your fear. Fear, like all other energy, will align with a vibration of similar frequency. If the fearful energy of your client finds a similar fear within yourself it could trigger an unresolved issue or karmic pattern to surface in you. You can tell whether or not such a thing has happened by the length of time it stays with you. If the discomfort stays with you for more than a few hours then you've probably taken it on. If this happens you have a wonderful opportunity to discover what the issue is and heal it. Once you shift your vibration at a core level, the discomfort will leave. No longer will your vibration be in alignment with that issue or wound. Like oil and water, they will separate and go their own ways. If the issue is not yours it usually passes within a few hours, or it's possible you may not feel it at all. Now, this is just a guideline put in a very general framework. There are many variables that could occur depending upon the knowledge, sensitivity , and inner capacity of the practitioner. For the average person though, keeping the doors open on the bottoms of your feet where minor chakras are located is a great way to allow unwanted energy to drain into the earth for cleansing. Calling on spirit guides, angels, Lords of Karma, or personal masters to assist in releasing, taking away, and purifying the energy is always a good idea. At the end of the day cleanse your energy field by smudging, dry bathing, pranic breath work, salt baths, or all of the above. Don't forget to cleanse the space where you work too. If you work with clients' everyday you should clear your chakras about once a month. This can be done by placing an object that will absorb energy, such as cotton cloth or crystal, on the front of each chakra touching the body. Exhale forcefully, both physically and energetically, any debris that is held there. These steps can spare you a lot of struggle if you follow them regularly.

If all of this seems too much or too frightening to deal with then it may be best to focus your Reiki skills only on yourself. If your desire

INTENTION

to help others truly comes from a place beyond the need for recognition or the desire (conscious or unconscious) to control, then there is no problem. Please take a close look at this and ask yourself why you are drawn to this work. Be honest. There is no dishonor in using Reiki just for yourself. Just because it's been taught as a way to help heal others doesn't mean you have to use it that way. It has also been taught as a self healing technique. One is just as valid as the other. In fact, in the end there is not an "other". Healing yourself is healing the world.

Unfolding to the gentle beauty that creates the Nature of Reiki can be a path by itself. You have seen from the information given up to this point, Reiki extends to all parts of our life. Discovering the wholeness from which these parts have their origin is to answer perhaps the only question we ever need to ask ourselves… "Who am I?" By consciously working with the Reiki energy through various meditations, exercises, chants, self discovery and dialogue processes, the unfolding truth of who you really are slowly blossoms into the radiant awareness that connects you to the joy of Life itself. For some, this can be more than enough. For others, the deep longing to be of service and support others in their healing is an important part in their journey. Such was the case with me.

The wounds I carried with me in this lifetime stayed well hidden from my sight until I was a middle aged adult. I have no doubt that others were able to see them clearly, but at the time I had no way to separate myself from them. Only when I began to see them as layers and patterns that existed on top of myself did I begin the process of healing. This process included, among other things, opening my heart to express the love I had successfully shut away for many many years. After such a long time I wasn't even sure what love was anymore. Slowly, by being patient with myself, allowing myself to make so called mistakes, and unfolding to the Reiki energies as outlined in these pages, I began to connect with other people in a more genuine way. A way which was

THE NATURE OF REIKI: A PATH OF INCLUSION

not looking for something in return. A way which allowed others to be who they were without wanting them to be another way. A way which helped open their hearts to heal their wounds. In other words, my journey was about healing the relationship I had with myself which led to genuinely wanting to share it with others. This longing to share was very strong because I knew that underneath the way most people were conducting their lives, they wanted to express more of their true nature too. I knew this because I asked them. For me, it seemed logical to include a hands on approach with Reiki since I already had training in massage therapy. Incorporating the Reiki deepened their massage experience to the degree that at one time many of my clients started using the term "Reikissage". I believe for many, as it is for me, the longing to serve and be of service brings deeper purpose to life. If you are one of those that have this longing, the following section offers ideas and specific techniques for following this path.

Use them as a starting point and guideline for fulfilling your desire to be of service. Allow your intuition to be heard and follow it to create your own unique approach and understanding of our complex nature. Enjoy your experience.

THE TECHNIQUES OF HEALING THROUGH REIKI

GETTING STARTED
"THE ENERGY BODY"

Feeling the energy body is greatly enhanced through the Reiki training and attunement process. But learning to identify that part of you can be started at any time. Here are a couple of exercises you can play with to help sense the non-physical you.

EXERCISE #3

With your hands about 16 to 18 inches in front of you, at head height, bring the tips of your index fingers lightly together. It helps to have a background color other than white. Now, keeping your focus on the center where the fingertips touch, slowly begin to pull them apart. Your field of vision will include your fingers as they separate, but your focus should remain centered. Look for the transparent white light that stays connected between them. You may also notice that the fingers themselves are surrounded by this same light. Take your time and relax your gaze, becoming fully present as you perform this exercise. It may take a few attempts so don't be discouraged if you don't see the light right away. It may also be helpful to change the background color if you're not having any luck. Once you see the energy in this manner you can begin playfully

THE NATURE OF REIKI: A PATH OF INCLUSION

experimenting by placing an index finger on any object and slowly pulling your finger away to view your connection. For example, I have a statue of Jesus meditating. By placing my index finger on his third eye and slowly pulling away I can see the light connected not only to my finger but also to an aura around his entire body. Try this with various objects such as plants, water, or even stones. Before you know it you'll be seeing energy fields around everything.

EXERCISE #4

Another fun exercise is to place your hands at shoulder height in front of you with palms facing each other. Slowly begin moving them toward the center of your body. As you do, you will begin to feel tangible sensations which characterize the energy. You might feel tingling like your hands had fallen asleep or like tiny electric shocks. You might also feel warmth or a magnetic "push-pull" sensation. Whatever you feel is perfect. The main point of this exercise is not to have a particular feeling or interpret what you feel, but rather to notice that you feel something. Anything that you feel is a quality of the life force.

By taking the time to sense these typically overlooked characterizations of our energy fields we begin to get grounded in a new dimension of being.

WORKING WITH ANOTHER "THE REIKI TREATMENT"

To start a traditional Reiki treatment a warm, comfortable room is recommended. Low lighting and soft colors help put people at ease right away, and the sound of running water from a fountain is often a welcome addition. While many people have sensitivities to aromas, the subtle fragrance of a pure essential oil or high quality incense can also add dimension to their experience. All in all, you want to create a full spectrum sensory experience for them if possible. Soft music to their liking and a gentle disposition from you, the practitioner, is sure to help them relax enough to open up and receive your heart offering. Hand positions and hand placement are great stepping stones to developing your intuition. Take your time and become comfortable with them. After a while you'll begin to sense the ever so slight variations of energy that will naturally guide you to experimenting and trusting your intuitive self.

It is always best to take a few minutes to center yourself before you begin your treatment. Open yourself to the infinite intelligence and feel your heart engaged – remember there is no "other". This is sacred work and should be honored as such.

Begin by having the person you are working on lie face up. Cradle their head in the palms of your hands until you feel energetic rapport

THE NATURE OF REIKI: A PATH OF INCLUSION

established. Ask the life force to move through your hands offering healing for the highest good. Some people like to say a little affirmation such as "Reiki flows freely through my life" or something similar to get going. One friend of mine simply says, "Reiki on". It may take a minute or two to begin to feel the flow of the life force moving through you. It may feel like tingling or a magnetic force field or some other sensation uniquely yours. The most common way however, is as heat. No one way is right or better than another, so however you feel it, just continue feeling it until that sensation begins to dissipate before you move to another part of the body. One of the most common mistakes is to hurry from one spot to the next. Slow down! If after two to three minutes you are not feeling anything, you can ask the person you are working on what they may be feeling. In the beginning it is not uncommon to overlook the subtle vibrations as they emanate from your hands. Sometimes the person receiving the treatment will be going through an intense journey while you are totally unaware that anything is happening. So, ask before you leave that area and move to the next. While three to five minutes is a pretty common time frame to keep your hands in one area, there have been many times that I could feel the life force flowing strongly for ten to twenty minutes without moving. Once you begin to feel it dissipate, then go on to the next.

There are a couple of ways to proceed with a full treatment once rapport has been established. You could scan the person's energy field by placing your hands one to eight inches above their body and slowly move from head to foot. As you do you will notice variations in what you feel. You may notice hot spots or cold spots or strong energy emanations that feel magnetic in quality. It's even possible to sense color or emotional qualities sometimes. Just take note of what you're sensing and choose a place to start. Typically, when I feel extreme heat on my palms I will start at the place where I felt that. To me this means the

WORKING WITH ANOTHER "THE REIKI TREATMENT"

area is calling for aide. Once those areas are addressed I might move to a cold spot.

A cold area typically indicates that the area is really blocked and needs to be opened up. Most of the time just laying your hands on or above the cold spot will begin to open it up. For that matter, the entire treatment can be given on or slightly above the body. This can be a great asset since some people find it uncomfortable to be touched. You may even come across someone who can't be touched such as a burn victim. Experiment and see which works for you.

Occasionally I sense the need to add one of the visualizations previously given in Exercise #1 & #2. There may be modifications needed to suit the situation, so be creative. Once the hot spots and cold spots have been addressed, let your intuition guide you toward completion.

Another way to begin is by starting at the head of the person after you have established energetic rapport described in the beginning of this section. A series of about 20 sequential hand positions will take care of most of the body.

THE NATURE OF REIKI: A PATH OF INCLUSION
HAND POSITIONS

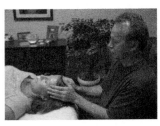

1. Start at the crown of the head with the base of your hands together and your fingers extending toward the ears.

2. Place your hands in a cupped position over each ear with your fingers pointing toward the feet.

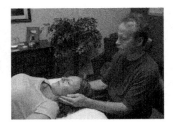

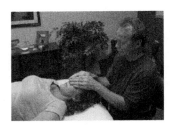

3. Place your cupped hands over each eye with your fingers pointing toward the feet.

4. Cup your hands with the fingers overlapping over the throat. Needless to say, be very gentle.

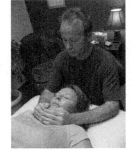

5. Ask the person you are working on if it is okay to place your hand over their heart. This is a vulnerable area for many people and just the asking will help bring comfort and instill a sense of your respect for them. If they say okay, then place your left hand under the neck and your right hand over their heart.

WORKING WITH ANOTHER "THE REIKI TREATMENT"

6. Place your hands over the front of the shoulders.

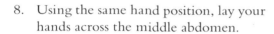

7. With the fingers of one hand touching the base of the other hand, lay your hands across the diaphragm.

8. Using the same hand position, lay your hands across the middle abdomen.

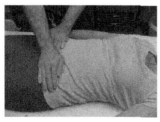

9. Lay your hands across the lower abdomen over the hip bones.

10. Place one hand over each knee.

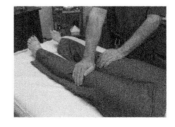

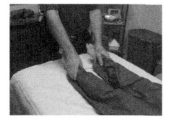

11. Standing at the feet, place one hand on top of each ankle.

THE NATURE OF REIKI: A PATH OF INCLUSION

12. Have the person turn face down and standing at their head, place one hand over each shoulder blade.

13. Using the same hand positions as you did for the abdomen, place your hands on the upper back.

14. Move to the middle back.

15. Place your hands over the lower back.

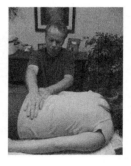

16. Place one hand over the back of the neck and the other hand over the sacrum.

17. Leaving one hand on the sacrum, move the other hand over the back of the heart.

WORKING WITH ANOTHER "THE REIKI TREATMENT"

18. Again, leaving your one hand on the sacrum, place the other hand over the crown.

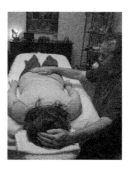

19. Place one hand over the back of each knee.

20. Place one hand on the sole of each foot.

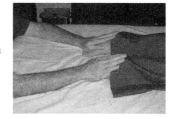

After you have completed the treatment, you may want to brush the aura from head to toe. This can be accomplished by "raking" the energy field using your fingers with both hands at the same time or by extending your dominant hand straight out with the thumb up creating a vertical circular motion from the head to the feet. The non-dominant hand simply holds the space as you move along. This not only brushes away residual energy that's been released but also gives a sense of closure.

Allow the person a few minutes to re-adjust and bring them a glass of water. Don't force the person to tell you what they experienced but gently ask; "Was there anything going on for you that you'd like to share, or do you have any questions?" Honor where they're at and encourage them to continue their journey in healing and/or consciousness expansion in whatever way they deem best. Let them know that while the treatment is over, the effects and impact of the experience will continue, however subtly, for at least the next few hours, maybe longer. Ask them to simply observe their emotional state for the rest of the day and perhaps pay special attention to their dreams that evening.

EXPLORING THE CHAKRAS AND MORE

One of the beautiful things about Reiki is that there are no hard, steadfast rules to follow in offering a treatment, save that your intention is for the highest good. This leaves endless passages and doorways to explore that allow you to get excited and create balance between the left and right brain. That is, between the analytical and intuitive; between knowledge and knowing. For example; the Chinese believe that disease starts in the joints. If you're inclined to step outside of the 20 hand positions you may feel drawn to place both hands around an elbow, an ankle, or any joint in the body. You might also want to include the use of essential oils or herbs in your treatment. Intending the energy of Reiki to pass through either one sends their healing properties deep into the body/mind. Here's a little secret that most people are unaware of. They don't even have to be out of the container to be effective. This is good news if you're working with someone who doesn't like the smell of a particular oil but could use the healing properties of the oil. The same principal applies to herbs. If you find one too distasteful to ingest you can place a poultice over the area you're seeking to balance and Reiki right through it. There are numerous books and healthcare professionals that can help you choose an oil or plant if you are drawn to using them. This can be a lifelong study in itself, so I won't delve too deep into their use as this would draw us too far off course.

A quick overview of what essential oils, plants, colors, and stones used during a treatment might be helpful. I have grouped them with our seven major chakras (energy centers) for a better sense of how they all work together.

WORKING WITH ANOTHER "THE REIKI TREATMENT"

Keep in mind that a wide range of vibrational energy is available within a single category or individual item within that category. For example, on the average, a single essential oil has over one hundred chemical constituents in it. This makes it versatile enough to be used for more than one thing. So if you see an oil, stone, or herb used in more than one Chakra it is because of this. I have purposely limited the items listed in a category to avoid confusion. Also, to separate the chakras without acknowledging the overlap of their energies carries the danger of not viewing the body as a whole. Please avoid doing this. It could be that a broken heart is responsible for far more than is listed within the category of the Heart Chakra. It could create a depression which lowers your immune response thus impacting your overall health. There really is no separation between the parts of ourselves, but I have broken it down this way so it's easier to view the predominant energies associated with them.

ROOT CHAKRA - (MULADHARA)

Location: The base of the spine.

Purpose: Links individual with the physical world.

Physical Effects: Circulatory system, reproductive system, spinal column, bones, teeth, nails, anus, rectum, colon, prostate and also influences testicles and ovaries, legs and feet, and pelvic areas of the body.

Emotional Effects: Revolve around basic body needs, safety, sexuality, space, security, boundaries and behavior around such factors set by culture.

In Balance: Creates deep connection with family, nature and trust in its law of ebb and flow.

Imbalance: Inability to trust nature and focuses on material possessions.

Essential Oils: Myrrh, Patchouli, Rosewood, Vetiver

Stones: Agate, Bloodstone, Garnet, Ruby, Smoky Quartz

Herbs: Burdock, white willow, astragalus

Inherent Color: Red

Associated body parts: Bones, teeth, nails, legs, arms, intestines, anus, prostate, vagina

SACRAL CHAKRA - (SVADHISTHANA)

Location: 2 to 3 finger-widths below the navel

Purpose: To balance the yang and yin energies – the male and female energies of creation and sexuality; balances the giving and receiving energies that underlie all relationships.

Physical Effects: Adrenal glands, reproductive system, muscular system, gonads, ovaries, prostate and testicles, regulates the female cycle, also effects kidneys and bladder

Emotional Effects: Feelings of trust, warmth, intimacy, attachments, addictions, creativity, and control.

In Balance: Enhances ability to share emotions, feelings, and the creative process with others.

Imbalance: Unable to express feelings, unsure of creative ability, and unbalanced sexual energy.

Essential Oils: Sandalwood, petitgrain, fennel, cinnamon, cardamom

Stones: Moonstone, carnelian, tourmaline

Herbs: Saw palmetto, calendula, Solomon's seal

Inherent Color: Orange

Associated body parts: Reproductive organs, kidney, bladder, ovaries, adrenals, colon, testes, and body fluids

SOLAR PLEXUS CHAKRA - (MANIPURA)

Location: Approximately 3 finger-widths above the navel

Purpose: To blend and integrate feeling and being; helps development of personal power and self esteem.

WORKING WITH ANOTHER "THE REIKI TREATMENT"

Physical Effects: Pancreas, stomach, liver, small intestine, blood sugar, digestion, adrenals and gall bladder, lower back, and autonomic nervous system

Emotional Effects: Will, personal power, balance. This chakra purifies the desires and wishes of the lower chakras and radiates as our emotional energy center.

In Balance: Creates strong sense of self esteem, self respect and discipline; brings feelings of wholeness and inner calm.

Imbalance: Creates fear of rejection, criticism, and mistrust of the natural flow of life.

Essential Oils: Chamomile, lemon, lemongrass, cedarwood, cardamom and thyme

Stones: Amber, citrine, tiger's eye, yellow topaz, agate

Herbs: Angelica, ginger, lemon balm

Inherent Color: Yellow

Associated body parts: Liver, gallbladder, spleen, pancreas, low back, abdomen, stomach, nervous system

HEART CHAKRA - (ANAHATA)

Location: Center of the chest

Purpose: To assist our emotional development in acting out of love and compassion. To help us recognize the most powerful energy we have is Love.

Physical Effects: Thymus gland and entire immune system, heart, circulatory system, and also relates to tissue regeneration, lymph and lungs

Emotional Effects: Lovingness, harmony, flexibility, ability to empathize and sympathize, allows for opening oneself to the cosmic vibration

In Balance: Creates feelings of love, compassion, forgiveness, inspiration, hope, acceptance and acts as a healing balm to self and others.

Imbalance: Creates fear of loneliness, commitment, and fosters insincerity; can bring about jealousy, bitterness and inability to forgive.

Essential Oils: Rose, bergamot, jasmine, geranium, clary sage

Stones: Emerald, rose quartz, and green jade

Herbs: Hawthorne, borage, American ginseng

Inherent Color: Green

Associated body parts: Heart, upper back, lower lungs, thymus, rib cage, circulatory system

THROAT CHAKRA - (VISHUDDHA)

Location: Throat, between inner collarbones

Purpose: To develop and express the alignment between our will and the will of God.

Physical Effects: Thyroid, parathyroid, mouth, teeth, sinus, allergies, ears

Emotional Effects: Serves as a bridge between our thoughts and feelings. Through this chakra we express our aliveness, our laughing and crying, our anxiety and aggressiveness, our love and happiness. It is also the center that enables us to hear our own inner voice, thus entering into contact with our inner spirit and become conscious of our real mission in life.

In Balance: Brings faith, self knowledge and expression of our "inner voice".

Imbalance: Fear of losing our personal will to the will of God; inability to find self expression; afraid of silence.

Essential Oils: Rosewood, spearmint, lavender, neroli

Stones: Aquamarine, turquoise, chalcedony

Herbs: Kava kava, yarrow

Inherent Color: Blue

Associated body parts: Thyroid, parathyroid, throat, upper lungs, voice, jaw

WORKING WITH ANOTHER "THE REIKI TREATMENT"

BROW CHAKRA - (AJNA)

Location: Between the eyebrows at the center of the forehead.

Purpose: To open the doors of intuition to becoming the seat of wisdom; to link knowing and being as one.

Physical Effects: Face, eyes, ears, nose, central nervous system, sinuses, pituitary gland and entire endocrine system

Emotional Effects: Our seat of attainment of consciousness. It is here we can manifest and de-materialize matter. This chakra also expresses itself in active and advanced intellectual skills. In other words, perception is greatly enhanced.

In Balance: May manifest clairvoyance, spiritual vision and an awareness that leads to universal connection.

Imbalance: Afraid to look within; fear of our shadow-self; fear of truth; only sees the obvious and surface meaning of events.

Essential Oils: Cedarwood, spruce, basil, rosemary, frankincense

Stones: Lapis lazuli, sodalite, indigo sapphire, opal

Herbs: Blue vervain, rosemary, ginkgo biloba

Inherent Color: Indigo

Associated body parts: Face, eyes, nose, sinus, pituitary gland, ears.

CROWN CHAKRA - (SAHASRARA)

Location: The top of the head

Purpose: To open our connection to the divine, to our own spiritual nature and transcendent dimension of being as pure consciousness.

Physical Effects: Pineal gland, hair, entire skeletal system, all nerve pathways and electrical synapse, hemispheric functioning of the brain

Emotional Effects: Manifests as compassion, at oneness, peace and nonattachment

In Balance: Brings full faith in the divine; develops qualities of trust, healing, and guidance beyond ordinary human experience.

THE NATURE OF REIKI: A PATH OF INCLUSION

Imbalance: Fear of spiritual abandonment, loss of identity, unable to imagine cosmic unity.

Essential Oils: Lavender, neroli, rosemary, frankincense

Stones: Amethyst, topaz, sugilite, fluorite, diamond

Herbs: Elder, damiana, artemesia vulgare (mugwort)

Inherent Color: Violet, white and gold

Associated body parts: Brain, skull, pineal gland

THE SYMBOLS

Symbols are used to communicate concepts and ideas. They were used before language developed but eventually evolved to represent language. Consequently, the older the language, the more fluid the concept or idea is. The Japanese kanji, from which the original Reiki symbols are derived, have their root in the Chinese kanji. The history of this language dates back to a time when people were connected with the fluidity of life; a time when understanding the slightest variables of conditions or perspective could mean life or death; understanding or not understanding. These important concepts were communicated through variations allowed for when creating the strokes of the symbols. It is for this reason that the Japanese kanji is suitable to represent the ancient concepts of healing inherent in the Reiki energy.

In our three dimensional world, everything is a symbol. Science has shown us that matter is not solid. Even the atom, which was once believed to be the solid building block of all matter, has been found to be mostly space. The world we live in is symbolic of the energetic world that lies beneath it. Each symbol has its own sacred purpose for life to evolve on this planet, ultimately connecting us to the source from which it all sprang. Indeed, every breath is a prayer, thoughts become things, and all life is sacred. For this reason, I am choosing to honor the intention of Dr. Usui by not placing the symbols themselves in this

THE NATURE OF REIKI: A PATH OF INCLUSION

book. They are sacred symbols of God's benevolent world existing as both conceptual and energetic aspects of the Divine Intelligence.

When a person who is not trained in Reiki is exposed to the symbols, more often than not the intellectual mind is engaged in trying to figure out how to use them. This is okay of itself but is only half of the equation. The symbol's energy cannot be fully understood or used by the intellect alone. The source, from which it sprang and is connected to, can only be accessed by a genuine commitment and openness on the part of the seeker. Probably the easiest way to make this commitment is by enrolling in a Reiki workshop. Here, your intention and commitment open the door to deeply attuning to the full spectrum of energies that each symbol represents. In fact, the Reiki attunement is a ritual of intent that activates your energy centers to accept the fullness of the symbols which then moves quickly through the subconscious to the super-conscious mind. No wonder so many people have been drawn to this beautiful energy of light and Love. In one short weekend, your commitment to expanding self awareness can be a life altering event. It's interesting to note that this approach to healing and self awareness has made itself known at such a crucial time on our planet. Science and spirituality are being drawn together to demonstrate the oneness of which we are all a part. It seems imperative that we continue to reach for a deeper understanding and experience of this oneness. Only in this way can we move forward to a golden age of peace unlike anything that has ever happened before on this planet.

Let's take a look at some of the specific symbols used in Reiki. Different schools may use variations of the same symbol, or in some cases even different symbols, as a part of their training. Each one offers insight into a particular aspect of the energy. In the original Usui system of Reiki there were four symbols. The modified system uses six symbols. The two additional symbols are some of those I spoke of earlier which predate language. Their discovery and inclusion into Reiki however, is

THE SYMBOLS

attributed to a system used by the Tibetans. There is no need to believe that because someone else is using a symbol different from the one you are using, that it is right, wrong, better, or worse. Intention is the key here. When you are exposed to the symbol during your training, a subconscious impression is created along with your understanding of its meaning. That impression is all you need be concerned with. <u>That</u> is the energy locked into the depths of your being. Deeper understanding of the symbol will come in time as you use and work with it, but not necessarily because of any variations. I strongly suggest that once you've been attuned to the symbols you use them in meditation. One way to do this is by simply holding an image of them (one at a time) in your mind's eye and feel the energy exchange between your energy field and the energy emanating from the symbol. Another way is by using the name of the symbol as a mantra. As you repeat the name of the symbol silently, imagine the fullness of its energy entering your body. These are just two ways you can help deepen your connection with their essence. Use your imagination and see what you come up with.

ACTIVATING THE SYMBOLS

Activating the symbols for use is simplicity itself. There are three basic ways to do this.

> *Physically draw the symbol in the air, imagining if you can,*
> *color and dimension.*
> *Say the name of the symbol out loud*
> *Simply visualize the symbol with your mind's eye*

Feel free to combine or even modify these steps if you're guided. For example, if you are working on a friend or client who is not trained in Reiki, you do not want to be waving your arms around repeating the names of the symbols out loud. They'll probably think you've lost your mind and go running in fear. In this situation it would be best to wait for them to relax and close their eyes before drawing out the symbols and say the names silently. If they choose not to close their eyes for some reason simply visualize the symbol and say the name silently.

Making your client comfortable is of utmost importance. Healing takes place when the mind and emotions are feeling safe and secure.

THE POWER SYMBOL

This symbol is used to increase the power of the Reiki energy. More specifically, it is used to symbolize the <u>essence</u> of power from Source. It is the backbone, or pillar of the omnipotent energy of the universe. The translation of this Kanji is a bit different than you'll find from other Reiki sources because it comes from a Chinese perspective. As I have mentioned before, the Japanese language is derived from the Chinese. Consequently, the definitions of the Kanji from the Chinese perspective often varied enough to give us a greater depth of understanding. This symbol means ***"The essence of the omnipotence beyond all."*** (Referring to a realm "vast and deep, beyond the mind") If you've already been trained in Reiki you've likely been told the translation of this symbol means "put the power here". At first glance there appears to be a conflict with the Chinese interpretation, but look a little closer. "Omnipotence" refers to the power of the universe. The essence of that power is purity with no judgment, no control. So, the purity, or essence, of the power that pervades the universe is what we are focusing on by activating this symbol.

Once this power is intended, an interesting thing happens. The increase of energy begins to vibrate so fast that it dislodges slower moving, stagnant energy and forms a barrier. This barrier then protects the area intended. It's as if you turn on a fan and the blades are moving so fast that there's no way to throw anything through the blades. You can use this symbol to clear an area and/or protect it. When giving a Reiki treatment, it is a good idea to first clear the room with this symbol by drawing a giant power symbol in the center of the room.

THE SYMBOLS

Then imagine the energy of the symbol dissolving and clearing away any negative energy that might be in the area. If you like, you can combine this exercise with other rituals of the same intention. For example, I will oftentimes draw out the symbol with a stick of high quality incense or a sage stick used for smudging. Picturing the symbol as three dimensional is also helpful, as is intending it to be a particular color. According to The Brotherhood for Healing, the inherent color of this symbol is red. But let me stress that you can choose any color you feel drawn to. The energy is alive and will work with slightly different character depending on the color you choose. Once you have cleared the room you will want to seal the walls, floor, and ceiling with the power symbol. This will keep unwanted energies from beyond your room from interfering with the work you are doing. Drawing a large power symbol in front of yourself and stepping into it can also be an empowering way to begin your treatment.

Once your client is lying comfortably with eyes closed, you can draw a large power symbol over their body with the center of the symbol being drawn over the abdomen. This will help dislodge stagnant or toxic energy they may be carrying on the surface. It will also help set the tone for the rest of the treatment. If you find an area on the body that feels exceptionally blocked you can draw the power symbol over that area and visualize the symbol sinking down into the body melting away the tension, stress or toxicity until the area begins to release. Once your treatment is complete, you can draw another power symbol over the entire body to seal it off from absorbing more negative energy once they leave.

Outside the session room the power symbol can be used in similar ways for other purposes. Basically, any time you want to clear, protect, or empower a particular area you can use the power symbol. Use it to protect your wallet, your car, your children (my wife used to slyly pat a power symbol on the back of our son as he was being sent off to school), your home, or any situation that calls for an increase of energy. Beware, using the power symbol without discernment may backfire. A great example of this happened to a close friend of mine who is a school teacher. One day she decided she was going to visualize a large Reiki power symbol hanging from the ceiling in her classroom. Her idea of course was to generate the Reiki energy so that the kids would behave. Unfortunately what happened was the opposite. The children became so charged with the energy that her day went up for grabs. Perhaps if she had used the Mental-Emotional symbol things would have been different. Let's take a look at that and see what you think.

THE MENTAL-EMOTIONAL SYMBOL

As the name implies, this symbol is used for balancing the mental-emotional energies within us. The Japanese translation for this kanji is **"Humanity and God become one."** The Chinese translation is **"To put together (or bring together) in harmony."** As you can see, this symbol is a quick way to step into the energy of balance. First, acknowledging an imbalance, we can see we are out of alignment with the truth of who we really are; that is, out of alignment with our "God Self". How do we know that we are out of alignment? By the way we feel. Our "God Self" is in perfect balance always. When we pinch ourselves off from this Self, we feel it as an angst, a judgment, depression, frustration, anger, or any other number of limiting possibilities that we humans experience. Activating the mental-emotional symbol we can quickly begin to rebalance ourselves. Whether it's an addiction, a self-worth issue, a relationship problem, or a broken heart, the mental-emotional symbol can help bring us back in alignment. Simply by drawing the symbol out in front of you and pulling it into your heart can be very effective. Try visualizing it as a combination of purple and violet to empower it even more. Another way would be to write a healing affirmation on a piece of paper along with the symbol and hold the paper over your heart while sending Reiki through it into your

THE SYMBOLS

heart. This way the essence of its vibration is given a chance to impact you on levels beyond conscious mind.

When working with a client, use this symbol with caution and compassion. There have been many times I have drawn this symbol over the heart and been met with a tearful response as their pain came pouring out. There is usually no need to offer advice. Just holding a safe loving space for the client to do their work and release those feelings is enough.

Again, working with affirmations can also be very effective while the client is receiving a standard Reiki treatment. For added dimension, place a drop of rose or jasmine oil on the paper. Its vibration will enhance the overall experience (unless of course your client doesn't like these aromas).

THE DISTANCE SYMBOL

This symbol has more variations in the way it is drawn than any other symbol in the Usui system. Regardless of how different they may be, it is used to send Reiki over time and space. Intention is the most important thing here. Relying on my Chinese friend Dr. Ming Te Lin, I discovered that the way I was originally taught, and continue to teach, the distance symbol means ***"The innate gift of my Being reaches the realm of my intention"*** (through the ability I am endowed with). The inborn or innate gift that the symbol refers to is the life force energy itself, the almighty power, and all the qualities of the divine in man. The Bible states that we are made in the likeness and image of God. In I Timothy 4:14 it says "Neglect not the gift that is in thee, which was given thee by prophecy, with the laying on of hands." So by our ability, we send the innate gift of our being, which is wholeness, to "The realm of our intention," which implies breaking all barriers of time and space since that realm is whatever or wherever our intention is.

A slightly quicker translation could be "I use the almighty power that I have been endowed with". Of course the implication would be sending this power into the past, future, place, or realm of intention.

THE NATURE OF REIKI: A PATH OF INCLUSION

I have to admit, that out of all the Reiki symbols in the Usui system, the distance symbol was the most challenging for me. Not because of its complex character as Japanese kanji, but because of its purpose. For many years prior to my Reiki training I had sent prayer to people around the world. I liken Reiki to a powerful prayer so I could not understand why I needed this symbol to do what I had already been doing. In fact, I was struggling so much with this conflict that I was getting ready to share it with my Reiki students one day. Then an odd thing happened. As I began to talk about the distance symbol, empowering words of why it was important began coming out of my mouth. It was as if somebody else had stepped into my body/mind and began speaking through me. I don't remember exactly what I said but I remember the feeling and general overview. It went something like this: "The conscious and subconscious mind limit our concepts of what is or what can be by focusing on past experience and conditioning. When we send prayer or healing energy over a distance, whether that distance be time or space, we generally have at least a subconscious restriction around its effectiveness. The ideas of time and space are the restriction! By using the distance symbol this restriction is bypassed because it allows us to work from the super-conscious state. The distance symbol quickly transports our intention through the conscious, the subconscious, and then into the super-conscious realm where the concepts of time and space are obliterated. In this space there is no resistance and your healing work can be truly effective." Well, I guess I told myself a thing or two. Anyway, ever since that day I have used the distance symbol with confidence and gratitude.

Its inherent vibration is golden yellow in color and can be used to transport our intention of healing, not only to a distant place, but also backward or forward in time. Many of us have wounded childhood memories that can be healed through connecting with the distance symbol. Send the healing energy of light and Love back to those times

THE SYMBOLS

along with your new understanding of knowing that each and every experience of your life has led you to the place you are today. See and feel the Reiki energy surrounding the situation and people involved. Sense the tension melting and offer forgiveness to all involved – including yourself, "for they know not what they do" (Luke 23:34). By the way, forgiveness does not mean that you condone the actions around a painful situation. Rather, you accept and understand the ignorance from which the actions originated. Forgiveness is for you. To stay attached to a painful situation only causes torment and eventually declining health in yourself. The distance symbol allows you to detach and lets the energy of Reiki do the work on a level beyond conscious thought.

If you are working on someone else, you can guide them to remember the situation they want healed and ask them to imagine a beautiful cloud of Reiki surrounding it. Tell them to sense the Reiki interpenetrating each and every cell, each and every molecule of their body and surrounding area. Guide them to feel the light and Love dislodging the pain and encouraging each person involved to speak their truth without judgment. When everyone has spoken, imagine the Reiki light becoming so bright and the feeling of love so intense that it consumes them and the entire situation back into the purity of pure spirit.

You can also send Reiki into the future by using this symbol. If, for example, you know you are going to be in a situation that normally causes stress (like a public speech or the dentist), you can send the healing energy of Reiki to that time and place by imagining the symbol radiating its energy (on the stage, podium, or dentist chair) with the intention that it release when you arrive. By the same token, you can connect with a client using the distance symbol and surround them with Reiki before they arrive at your office if you feel it would be helpful. Again, there are no limits to how you can use this symbol. Imagination is the key.

THE NATURE OF REIKI: A PATH OF INCLUSION

THE MASTER SYMBOL

The Usui Master Symbol is the fourth and final symbol of the original Usui system. As such, it is intended to help the student get in touch with their mastership. It is about claiming the master within. And while this is a never-ending process of unfolding, it is imperative that we learn to embrace the greater truth of who we really are. Only in this way can we take responsibility for our life and begin to know ourselves as co-creators.

There are several definitions which aptly fit the Japanese kanji. "Great being of the universe, shine on me, be my friend" is the most common definition. "Treasure House of the Great beaming light" is the definition stated in the Encyclopedia of Eastern Philosophy and Religion[s2]. And in some Zen circles, it is used as an expression of one's own Buddha-nature. In other words, it is the light of the universe embodied in us and shining forth our true nature. In Christian terms, it is about claiming the truth I AM. If you recall the Bible verse Exodus 3:14, where Moses is talking to God, symbolized as the burning bush, Moses asks God, "And who shall I say has given me these words?" God Replies, "Tell them I AM hath sent you". Now you can imagine Moses going to the people of Israel and saying "The God I AM has sent me to tell you these things..." You can see very quickly that <u>that</u> "I AM" is God. Who can say such a thing except each and every one of us for ourselves? In other words, God has told us his/her name (nature) is "I AM". In doing this God cleverly told us that each and every one of us is "Made in the image and likeness of God", Genesis 1:27. We are all God's light shining forth on this earth. The Christ Consciousness and/or Buddha Nature are embodied in each and every one of us.

By combining the definitions of the Usui Master Symbol together and affirming the truth given to us in the Bible, the definition of this powerful symbol is ***"Great Light of the Universe enters my Crown***

THE SYMBOLS

Chakra and Manifests as me on Earth.'' Or another way to say it would be "I AM the light of the universe".

The Usui Master Symbol is a symbol to remind us of, and taps into, this universal truth that is encoded deep within the subconscious and super-conscious aspects of our being. Use this symbol first to encompass and empower the other symbols. In this way you enhance their qualities by adding the high vibration inherent in its nature. And just as important, you add and connect to the process of intention by claiming your truth as a son or daughter of God. When the meaning of this symbol is truly realized, not intellectually theorized you can throw away this book and quit searching.

For this reason, I strongly suggest that you meditate daily with this symbol. There are endless ways to do this so I'll give one example as a possibility. Draw out the Master symbol as if it were lying flat on a plate made of pure energy. Imagine the plate with the symbol sitting on the top of your head. Putting your tongue on the roof of your mouth, breathe in to the sound and rhythm of its first two syllables as you imagine light streaming down through your crown and capturing the energy within the symbol. Breathe this light energy down your spine all the way to the root chakra while silently sounding the last syllable of its name. Imagine all of the light energy being spread into your body. It may help you visualize the light a little easier if you imagine the color of the light as a combination of purple and white. Do this for at least 5 minutes or up to 15 minutes each day.

As your energy begins to acclimate to this new vibration you will begin to sense shifts that impact your overall well-being. A greater feeling of peace, balance, and vitality are often among the benefits.

THE TIBETAN SYMBOLS

In the modified Usui system that we teach, there are two Tibetan symbols which empower and enhance the entire Usui system of healing. They create a quick and powerful link to the higher vibrations of Reiki,

THE NATURE OF REIKI: A PATH OF INCLUSION

thus condensing the time it takes to acclimate yourself to your Self. I mentioned earlier that they do not have an exact translation because they predate language, and most of the time they are used in conjunction with the attunement process. However, once you're exposed to their energy it's easy to see how they could be used in other ways. One of them acts as a vessel to direct and charge the Reiki energy as it enters the body. The other acts as a pathway for the energy to distribute itself so as to not go into overload. These powerful symbols have been incorporated into Reiki as a sign of the times. A time when the quickening of light and Love on this planet is needed as the foundation for the beginning of a new Golden Age.

Once you have learned the symbols, you can use them not only with people, but with plants, animals, stones, and the earth itself.

Have fun! These symbols were created to help ground the Reiki energies within the earth of which we are a part. Using a physical representation of the energies helps our limited minds to open to the wonder of spiritual energy. But remember, of themselves the symbols do not hold power. Our accepting and stepping into the energies is the power. Use it always for the highest good.

STEP BY STEP SESSION INSTRUCTIONS

I thought it might be helpful to go over some of the possibilities for a Reiki session in a step by step sequence. I would like to stress the word "possibilities" because there are as many ways to approach a session as there are people. Yet, the following guidelines may be useful in their own right, or may become the springboard for new ideas of your own. I will approach only two variations within the theme of healing; one for a physical ailment and one for emotional pain. As you know, the two are most often related but your client may not know that. To put the client at ease, address their concern as quickly as possible before opening up the possibility of adjunct approaches.

PHYSICAL HEALING

Lets say that your client comes to you for a pain in their abdominal area. Upon viewing their intake form along with some discussion, you discover that they are aware that when they eat certain foods the pain seems to intensify. This in turn distracts them from being present, available, and productive in other areas of their life. They tell you they are in pain right now so you ask them: "If the number 10 represented the most severe pain and the number 1 represented no pain, at what level would you rate the pain right now?" They answer 6. You remember reading in the chakra section of this book that yellow and orange were the colors associated with this area of the body. You also remember

101

THE NATURE OF REIKI: A PATH OF INCLUSION

reading in the affirmation section that there are a couple of affirmations that may be helpful for this condition.

Ask them to sit for a minute while you reference affirmations that may be helpful for their condition. You open to "Affirmations for Physical Healing (General Overview)" and browse through. You feel that jumping into the "I AM" affirmations may be a stretch for them without at least a little explanation. So you explain to them that recently (or not) you were reminded that in Christian teachings, the Bible says that the name for God is "I AM". Understanding that God is everywhere, even within each and every cell of your body, you can claim the "I AM" within. Since the "I AM" is perfect balance, holding an "I AM" affirmation in mind while receiving their treatment will help balance their energy field for greater alignment. You explain that you too will be holding the affirmation creating an even more powerful field of possibility. "Jesus said 'where two or more are gathered in my name (that is, the name of absolute Love or Christ nature) there I am also." You can choose a nice, gentle affirmation that can easily apply to this situation. For instance: "I acknowledge and embrace the living expression of radiant health I AM". Make sure they can resonate with the statement before continuing. If for some reason they cannot then perhaps they can create one that feels more comfortable to them. If not, you can simply proceed without the affirmation. If we assume for the sake of this illustration that they can accept the affirmation, then our next step is to write it out on a piece of paper and ask them to lightly hold the paper in their hand while they are receiving treatment.

Once they have memorized the statement you ask them to lay face up on your table, close their eyes, and relax while you center yourself. Hopefully you'll have already created an inviting atmosphere as mentioned in the section on Intention. Close your eyes and bring your awareness to that place inside yourself that feels peace. That place where you feel the life energy of the universe moving through you

STEP BY STEP SESSION INSTRUCTIONS

and through all life as one organism. Take a deep breath and allow the intelligence of that life to fill your body and mind. Now, ask for guidance. Ask your angels, Reiki masters, and Reiki guides to assist you with the healing. Acknowledge that your intuition is connected with them and give thanks. If you haven't already done so, seal the walls, floor, and ceiling with the power symbol. This can be done by simply drawing them in the air if your client still has their eyes closed. If not, you may want to ask them to close their eyes and focus on their affirmation while you set the energies in the room, or you could simply visualize the symbol. Next, draw or visualize the master symbol followed by the power symbol on your palms and on the top of your head. Draw a life size master symbol over the client's body followed by a large power symbol ending over the stomach and begin your treatment. In this case, you may first want to get a small piece of citrine and carnelian out of your bag of chakra stones. They will assist in the alignment of the second and third chakras into vibrational balance. Now, to add dimension and more vibrational alignment, place a drop of lemongrass (for the 3rd chakra) and a drop of fennel (for the 2nd chakra) on the palms of your hands. Place the stones over the abdomen and your hands over the stones while offering Reiki. As mentioned in the section "Working with Another", it sometimes takes a minute or two before the Reiki flows at maximum force, so be patient. You should begin to feel the heat, tingling, or whatever sensation you experience when offering Reiki, building to an intensity within a short while.

Maintain your hand position until you begin to feel the energy dissipate. Then, unless you are guided to do otherwise, move to the head and begin a full treatment using all the hand positions as indicated in the section "Working with Another". A full treatment will generally last between 45 and 90 minutes. When the client flips onto their stomach, pay extra attention to the area between the twelfth thoracic vertebra and the third lumbar vertebra. This area holds the nerves that regulate

THE NATURE OF REIKI: A PATH OF INCLUSION

the abdominal region of the body. (Refer to "General Overview of Body/Spine Relations" chart on page 108.) When you get to the feet you may want to, once again, spend a little extra time here since they contain reflex points relative to the organs, chakras, and other parts of the body. It's not necessary that you know reflexology for you to be effectively working on the feet. Just knowing that these points are there is enough for now. If you desire to learn more about reflexology there are numerous books available to you at the bookstore or library. To go into too much detail about this is beyond the scope of this book. But adding another drop or two of essential oil to your palms (or client's feet if they're bare) can be helpful at this point. The Reiki energy will infuse the healing properties of the oil into the reflex points of the affected area on the bottoms of the feet providing a more focused spectrum of energy that will enhance the treatment.

When finished, draw a large power symbol over their back and ask them to turn over. Brush the aura from head to toe and once again place a large power symbol over the body. Ask them to remain relaxed while you go get them a glass of water. When you return, help them to sit up and ask them about their experience. Worst case scenario would be that they didn't experience anything except relaxation. That's perfectly okay. If that's the case, explain to them that when they are relaxed, the immune system has a chance to recharge and become more effective in combating their illness or pain. Best case scenario is that they've had an hour of insights, body awareness of healing energy, and a kaleidoscope of vibrant colors in their mind's eye. Whichever the case, ask them, "On a scale of 0 to 10 – 10 being the most pain, at what level pain do you feel now?" Make sure you mark it on their intake sheet next to the pain level of when they arrived.

EMOTIONAL HEALING

For this example, we're going to look at healing a broken heart. It seems to be a common issue that plays itself out in just about every

STEP BY STEP SESSION INSTRUCTIONS

human being at one time or another. There are endless variations around the particulars so we're going to have to generalize a lot. For example, if someone lost their child it would probably be different than if the same person broke up with their lover. The one thing that both situations would probably have in common is the broken heart. So that is what we're going to focus on.

Set the energies in your room as mentioned in the section on physical healing. When your client comes in, offer them a chance to verbally express their grief. When they are complete, ask them to rate their level of pain from one to ten; ten being the most pain. Mark it down on your intake sheet. Open your compassionate heart to them but be careful not to take on their pain. Empathy, not sympathy is the key for achieving this. Even with an empathetic intention, it's best to imagine that doors on the bottoms of your feet have opened up allowing any energy from them to drain out the opening into the earth. Don't worry, Mother Earth can take care of it. Part of its purpose is to recycle old energies and purify them. If you've ever experienced hot spring healing waters you know what I'm talking about. It's only after water has journeyed through the earth for many years that it surfaces with this unique characteristic. So taking the fearful or negative energies from your client is not a problem and will not pollute the earth in the way you might be thinking. Simply be present to them and know that they are probably telling themselves some kind of story like "It should never have happened that way" or "If I had done such and such none of this would ever have happened". Understand and give them the space to feel what they feel while holding to your understanding that life happens the way it's supposed to. It's our arguing with it that causes most of the pain. So your intention is going to be helping them align with life and feel the Love they hold as the dominating vibration over pain. For what is this pain except the feeling of Love expressed in reverse? Help them to feel the Love that is the foundation of their sorrow. You do this by

THE NATURE OF REIKI: A PATH OF INCLUSION

simply holding a space of Love within yourself; a space of compassion; a space of trust.

Suggest that they contemplate the affirmation for loss and grief as follows: "The all pervading spirit of universal Love brings me to see the depth of Love I AM through this loss". Explain that "I AM" is the name God has identified with in the Bible. Write the affirmation out on a piece of paper. If appropriate, you can draw the distance symbol on the paper too. This is the symbol that your intention is to go beyond the boundaries of limited consciousness which is relative to time and space. You may also want to draw the mental/emotional symbol too. If your client has not been trained in Reiki, you can simply draw them out in the air and/or visualize them. I say this because they may want to take the paper home. If available, place a drop of jasmine and/or sandalwood on your palms before you begin your treatment. You might also consider placing the oils on the paper with the affirmation.

After they lie down and close their eyes, begin your treatment by asking them to imagine that there is a door over their heart. Instruct them to open the door and allow the pain to be released through the door. Explain that they may see the pain as dark clouds or murky water flowing out more and more until it <u>feels</u> as if it is all gone. Give them ample time for this to occur. Once they have told you that it has all been released, have them close the door. Now, place the paper with the affirmation over their heart and begin to let the Reiki flow through the paper into their heart. Ask your client to imagine that the radiant warmth they are feeling has a beautiful green hue to it; a green that reminds them of the balance and renewal they feel when they are in nature. Have them see and feel the green color penetrating every cell, and even the space between the cells of their heart. Imagine the green creating a beautiful aura of peace within and around their chest.

Once the foundation of release, renewal and peace has been created, move to the head and begin a standard treatment. Make sure to use the

STEP BY STEP SESSION INSTRUCTIONS

mental/emotional symbol around their head as this will help create balance in their thoughts. Once they have flipped onto their stomach, focus on balancing the heart and head before you move to the remaining hand positions. This can be done by placing a drop of frankincense on the palm of your left hand and a drop of jasmine on your right hand. Stand to the side of your client so that your right hand is over the area of the heart and your left hand is over their crown. Now, just hold your hands there allowing the Reiki to flow through connecting the two centers together. Try not to control or force the direction of the energy. The Intelligence within the Reiki will take care of that all by itself. When this feels complete, begin the standard hand positions until finished.

After you've gotten them a glass of water and they're sitting up, ask them about their experience. Ask them to rate the level of pain from one to ten; ten being the most severe pain, and compare it to the number they gave you before the session began.

Remind them once again that Love is all there is. It's when we pinch our self from that Love that we suffer. Pain may not be avoidable but suffering is optional. By continuing to focus only on the loss, we deny ourselves the balance which comes from seeing why we feel the loss to begin with.

General Overview of Body/Spine Relations

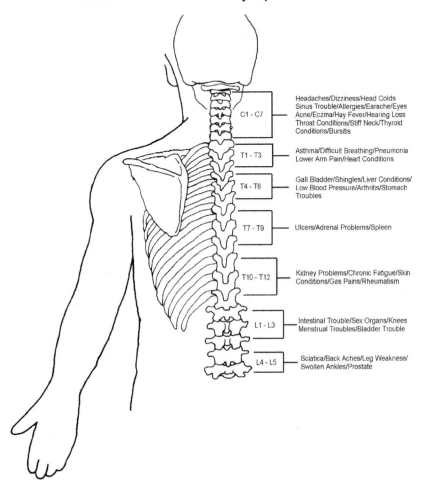

CONCLUSION:
THE EVER PRESENT JOY OF REIKI

A PATH OF INCLUSION

All enlightened groups of people, organizations, or civilizations, were created on the foundation of inclusiveness. An in depth look at history clearly shows this to be true, although there may be some discussion around the definition of enlightened. Living in separation has never really worked for large groups and exclusivity has never really worked for the individual. The world today is naturally heading toward inclusion. Most of the major world powers have political and economic systems that not only interact with one another but depend on this interaction. Even spirituality is crossing boundaries as more and more people realize that religious divisions have only created conflict. Growing numbers of people are turning to groups that think outside the box of "our way is the only way." Organizations such as The First Church of Religious Science, Unity, Unitarian, Self Realization Fellowship, The Isha Foundation, and many more are creating the foundation of a peaceful world. None of these groups ask you to give up your religion but rather to nurture it to the point of embracing all religions like Jesus, or Krishna, or the Buddha embraced every human being. Major publications like Eckhart Tolle's "The Power of Now" and Neal Donald Walsch's "Conversations with God" series have helped open millions of minds to greater possibilities in living. Oprah Winfrey alone has helped shift the consciousness of countless people around the

THE NATURE OF REIKI: A PATH OF INCLUSION

world. By focusing on loving, accepting, and self empowering inclusive concepts, the average person sitting in their living room has become aware of a whole new way of being.

The difficulty that still confronts us however is that most of these great possibilities being offered are kept in the conceptual world. Thinking about them and living them are two different things. Reiki offers a solution. Not the only solution, but a solution that may appeal to you if you're looking for inner freedom. Reiki is a path of inclusion. It can lead you to the four corners of the earth and back again. It is your connection to life, all life. When we immerse ourselves in the foundational building blocks of light and Love, life begins to shine with a brilliance that seems new and awesome. This brilliance has always been there, but through the proper Reiki training, it is once again felt and seen in ever increasing waves of awareness. Living becomes magical, the unknown less fearful. Helping one another comes naturally and guidance on our journey ever available.

The hands on approach to using Reiki has been accepted worldwide. Thousands of people are now reaching out to share this beautiful healing energy. Thanks to the efforts of Dr. Usui and all those who have embraced his work, the light of Reiki has been successfully grounded on our planet. People from all walks of life are beginning to benefit from its use, as indicated by its availability through a growing number of hospitals, hospice programs, and health care professionals. Moms and dads have always and intuitively reached out to place their hand over an injured site on their children. Now they have a framework around their action, which through Reiki training, can be enhanced tremendously. It looks like the awareness of Reiki is here to stay. Yet, underneath its acceptance and use, a developing phenomenon has been emerging. Deeper and deeper layers of conditioning and wounds are being brought to the surface for the practitioner. Some of these issues and wounds can be healed without conscious awareness. Some though,

A PATH OF INCLUSION

must become conscious in order to live life in alignment. The time has come to open up, face the fears and walk the talk. A commitment to understanding the nature of Reiki will serve you in doing just that. Whether addressing conscious or unconscious issues in life, the beauty inherent in this energy will guide you safely through its twists and turns. As these deep wounds and hidden issues surface for healing, they can be brought to the altar of light and Love to expose the truth and change your life forever. Using Reiki for self empowerment, self healing, and self awareness is a powerful approach which has not garnered the same attention as helping others. I encourage you to shift your attention in this direction if you haven't already. There are new worlds waiting to be explored. New ways of being which will lead to greater and greater benefits for everyone. We have only just begun to tap into this multi-dimensional energy.

My wish for you, for me, and for all of mankind is to be able to touch this grace so fully that the golden rule (Do unto others as you would be done by) no longer has to be considered, but known in the depths of our heart as the only way to live… because it is.

ABOUT THE AUTHOR

John David Sparks began his metaphysical studies in 1972. His thirst for spirit led him to many different teachings including Science of Mind, Self Realization Fellowship, Transcendental Meditation, the Arica Institute, and more.

In 1990 he became a massage therapist which led him to taking his first Reiki class in 1991. This quickly became his new passion and in 1994 completed his training in the Usui system. Shortly after this, with unexpected help, he founded Insight Awareness Center in the south suburbs of Chicago. Through the many years of working intensely with Reiki energies he realized that it is much more than just a hands-on healing technique. It is the core and essence of who we are connecting us with the core and essence of all living things. It is, when rightfully embraced, a path leading to a never ending, ever expanding experience of our divinity.

John is not aligned with any particular religion, although his early background was largely Christian. He teaches that Reiki transcends all religions and works at igniting the fire within each individual to inspire them in passionately finding and following their own unique way to peace.

Besides occasional international speaking engagements and Reiki retreats, he is currently teaching Reiki on a regular basis with co-owner of Insight Awareness, Valerie Reilly.

For information about Reiki classes scheduled, to sponsor a Reiki class in your area or for more information about an in depth Reiki Training as a Life Path contact:

John David Sparks
Insight Awareness
18110 Martin Ave.
Homewood, IL 60430
708-957-1284
john@insightawareness.com

RECOMMENDED READING

- Reiki Fire by Frank Arjava Petter: *Lotus Light Publishing, 1997*
- The Original Handbook of Dr. Mikao Usui, by Mikao Usui and Frank Arjava Petter: *Lotus Light Publishing, 1999*
- The Hayashi Reiki Manual, by Frank Arjava Petter, Tadau Yamaguchi, Chujiro Hayashi: *Lotus Press Publishing, 2003*
- Reiki The Healing Touch, by William Lee Rand: *Vision Publications, 2005*
- The Spirit of Reiki, by Walter Lubeck, Frank Arjava Petter, William Lee Rand: *Lotus Light Publishing, 2000*
- The Hidden Messages in Water, by Masaru Emoto: *Beyond Words Publishing, 2004*
- The Power of Now, by Eckhart Tolle: *Namaste Publishing, 1999*
- Loving What Is, by Byron Katie: *Harmony Books, 2002*
- Dark Side of the Light Chasers, by Debbie Ford: *Berkley Publishing, 1998*
- Conversations With God Series, by Neal Donald Walsch: *Hampton Roads Inc., starting 1996*
- A New Earth, by Eckhart Tolle: *Namaste Publishing, 2005*
- Autobiography of a Yogi, by Paramahansa Yogananda: *Self Realization Fellowship Publishing*
- The Divine Name, by Jonathan Goldman: *Hay House, 2010*

Printed in Great Britain
by Amazon